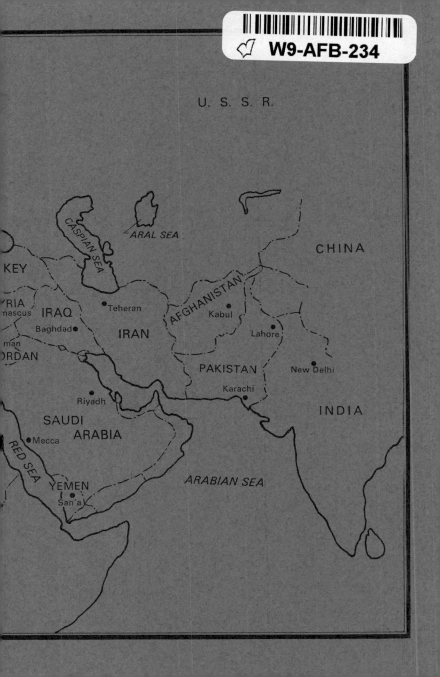

W9-AFB-234

U. S. S. R.

CASPIAN SEA

ARAL SEA

CHINA

KEY

RIA
nascus

Teheran

IRAQ

Baghdad

IRAN

AFGHANISTAN

Kabul

Lahore

man
ORDAN

PAKISTAN

New Delhi

Karachi

Riyadh

SAUDI
ARABIA

INDIA

Mecca

RED SEA

ARABIAN SEA

YEMEN

San'a

Understanding
the Middle East

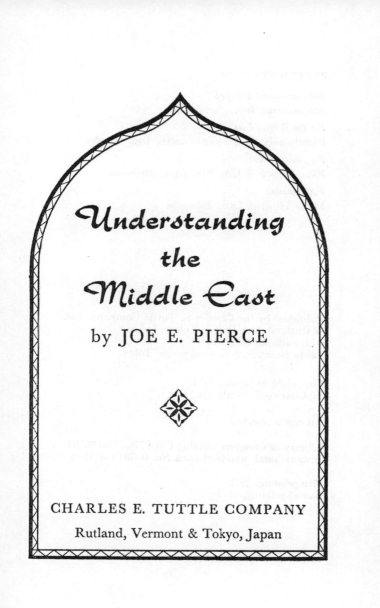

Understanding
the
Middle East

by JOE E. PIERCE

CHARLES E. TUTTLE COMPANY
Rutland, Vermont & Tokyo, Japan

REPRESENTATIVES

For Continental Europe:
BOXERBOOKS, INC., *Zurich*

For the British Isles:
PRENTICE-HALL INTERNATIONAL, INC., *London*

For Australasia:
PAUL FLESCH & CO., PTY. LTD., *Melbourne*

For Canada:
M. G. HURTIG, LTD., *Edmonton*

Published by the Charles E. Tuttle Company, Inc.
of Rutland, Vermont & Tokyo, Japan
with editorial offices at
Suido 1-chome, 2–6, Bunkyo-ku, Tokyo

Library of Congress Catalog Card No. 70–158787
International Standard Book No. 0–8048–0670–5

First printing, 1971
Second printing, 1972

PRINTED IN JAPAN

*With much love
to my son David and my daughter Carol,
who throughout their lives have been a joy,
a delight, and a pain in the neck.*

Table of Contents

List of
Illustrations

CHAPTER ONE

A Pluralistic Culture

This book is intended to be an introduction to the values of the peoples of the Middle (or Near) East, a geographic area which is many different things to different people. Political scientists, geographers and historians may all have slightly different regions in mind when they use this label. To an anthropologist the Middle East is a culture area.[1] *Culture* includes almost everything that mankind has and does that is not biologically inherited; that which is learned or created and passed on to succeeding generations.[2] This includes, among many other things, political systems, methods of warfare, agricultural techniques, language, art motifs, clothing styles, etc. Thus a culture area is a geographic region wherein the cultures of the communities all have a common quality or flavor. This is not to say that all of the cultures are the same; they may be very different in the specific details of their patterned ways of life, but still they seem to have an over-all quality about them which is very similar,

11

especially when they are compared with communities in neighboring areas. For example,
threshing is done by some villages in the Middle
East with a wooden sled which looks much like a
short toboggan with tiny flakes of obsidian or flint
imbedded in the underside of it. This device cuts
into the stalks of wheat as it is ridden over them and
frees the grain.[3] Other villages in the same area use
a vehicle with knife blades attached to its wheels to
do the same job.[4] Despite these observable variations (and hundreds of small items such as these
could be cited), the agriculture of the villages is
based on small grains, and the life which subsists
mainly on this agricultural pattern has for the most
part a very similar quality from village to village all
the way from West Pakistan and the Punjab in
India to Morocco at the far western end of North
Africa. This similarity is the basis for considering
the Middle East to be an area which encompasses
Morocco, Algeria, Tunisia, Libya, Egypt and a
large strip across the northern Sudan in North
Africa, Saudi Arabia, Jordan, Israel, Yemen, Aden,
Syria, Afghanistan, West Pakistan and part of
northwestern India as well as some transition areas
surrounding this core.

Since sub-cultures have been mentioned, we
should say something about them. On the basis of
language and certain other cultural differences
(e.g., clothing styles) the strip of Asia which includes Turkey, Iran, Afghanistan and Pakistan can
be set off from the remainder of the area. Linguisti-
cally, this section is dominated by groups speaking

Turkic and Indo-European languages rather than Hamito-Semitic. While the area outlined above can be set off from the rest of the Middle East, the coasts of Turkey along the Mediterranean Sea, the Dardanelles, the Sea of Marmara and the Black Sea as well as the Caspian coast of Iran and the marshes of the Euphrates River also have sub-cultural differences which separate them from the others in the region. We can thus classify these as sub-subcultural areas.

Carleton S. Coon has coined the term "mosaic"[5] for the particular configuration of sub-cultures which exists in the Middle East. This is a brilliant insight into the relationship which exists between groups within the area. The concept of mosaic suggests that the area can best be discussed as if it were composed of three culture types with elements from each scattered over the same section of the earth's surface as opposed to the usual situation wherein the sub-areas occupy mutually exclusive territories. It explains why the difference between Ankara and Baglum, a village ten kilometers from the city, is very great despite the geographic proximity, because the city belongs to one type of culture while the village belongs to another. Similarly the differences in culture between the villages in Iran and the nomadic tribesmen who migrate around them are very great, again because the nomadic peoples belong to one type of culture and the settled villagers to another.

If one were to assign a color to each ethnic group in the Middle East (i.e. Kurds, Jews, various

Bedouin tribal groups, Turks, etc.) and a shade of the same color to each sub-cultural group within these units, he could then paint the geographic area occupied by each group with that color, and the region would appear on a map as a mosaic picture. However, Coon refers to more than just what is demonstrated by this graphic device. In a mosaic each small piece of the picture is a unit, in a sense independent, yet each forms a part of a larger whole. Fundamentally this means that the many ethnic groups that have crossed and recrossed the Middle East in the migrations of centuries of invaders have not been blended into a relatively homogeneous culture but rather have been integrated into a functioning whole, a pluralistic culture, without losing their specific sub-cultural identities.

Coon suggests that there are three sub-areas, which he sees as superimposed one on top of the other. First, and basic, are the food producers. The largest number of these are the settled villagers. The villagers are completely self-sufficient and could exist, but not without some deprivation, without the other elements in the mosaic. The second group is comprised of the various nomadic herding cultures. Some of these could live completely dependent on their herds alone, but many could not without reducing their populations, and the diets of the people would have to be restricted and shorn of much of their present variety. The third cultural type is represented by the urban centers. The cities are, of course, almost wholly dependent on the other two sub-cultures, i.e. the villagers and no-

mads, for their food supply. The cities are little
mosaics within the larger picture. For example,
Raqqa, a city in northern Syria, is occupied princi-
pally by settled Nomads, mostly Bedouin, but from
different tribal groups. If on a map each tribe's
urban area were colored differently, denoting that
their cultures are somewhat different, one could
see that the city is divided into sections, each of
which is occupied by a particular tribe. In addition
there would be one section which contains the
government offices as well as people affiliated with
no tribe. Here the culture would be somewhat
different from that of the settled nomads, and this
would be represented by still another hue. The
residents know which parts are controlled by which
tribes, and members of unfriendly tribes do not
wander freely in and out of each other's sectors.
The mosaic concept thus points out the semi-
autonomous nature of the cultural groups, yet an
overview of the picture thus created illustrates the
tight interdependence of each group on all the
others. The city must have cereal foods from the
villages and meat from the nomadic herdsmen, and
both the nomads and peasants want such things as
metal tools and luxuries which are produced only
in the cities. Within the cities it is common for each
ethnic or tribal group to specialize as to occupation,
e.g., Jews are merchants, Armenians are goldsmiths,
etc. Therefore, it is to everyone's advantage not to
kill off the Jews, Turks, etc., no matter how much
one might dislike them, and as a result, a tenuous
sort of stability is maintained by a mutual depen-

dence. Needless to say, this delicate balance breaks down when emotions are stretched too far. Hence, these cultural manifestations are important factors in the instability of the power alignments in the Middle East.

1. Biblos, a ruin near Beirut, Lebanon. Traces of Phoenician, Roman, Greek and medieval cultures are superimposed on one another here.

2. Roman ruins along the coast of Lebanon. The Romans were one of several groups which have controlled parts of the Middle East and contributed to its culture.

3. One of the earliest known Aryan tombs in Pakistan. The Aryans (or Indo-Europeans) invaded Pakistan and upper India from Persia about 3,000 years ago.

4. Aya Sofia, Istanbul. The structure dates from the 3rd
century A.D., when it was used as a church. Under the

Turks it became a mosque, and in the mid-1920s it
was converted into a national museum.

5. Restaurant east of Ankara. For centuries travelers have stopped at this spot to rest under the shade of a great tree and drink the water flowing from a spring inside its trunk.

6. Typical Mideast rural scene, with village home. The piles of manure shown here are used as fuel for cooking and heating; in the distance are the fields farmed by the villagers.

7. The Turkish village of Baglum. Cultural groupings are more important than territorial divisions in accounting for the great differences between this village and the city of Ankara, only ten miles away.

8. Village in Jordan. Here, and throughout the Mideast, the villagers raise the wheat and other agricultural products needed by the nomads and city dwellers.

9–12. Turkish threshing scenes. Plates 11 and 12 show the sled with sharp flint spikes used to cut up the stalks and help separate the wheat. Similar processing techniques are used throughout the Mideast.

13. Typical mountain desert scene. Most Mideast deserts are rocky or mountainous, with little fuel or water, sparse pasturage and extreme cold at high altitudes.

14. Turkish mountain peasants. The hostility of their environment is matched by that of the nomad tribesmen who in the past stole their crops and threatened their water supplies.

15. Loaded camels. The camel nomads have more freedom of movement than other herding people because camels can go for several days without water.

16. Sheep in a typically barren landscape (13th-century Turkish bridge in background). These sheep are being brought to drink at the banks of the Kizilirmak River in Turkey.

17. City street in Sinope, Turkey. Such a city usually contains skilled artisans of several different cultural groups, occupying different urban sectors.

18. Street scene in Karachi, Pakistan. These homes belong to refugees from the border regions who streamed into the city following the partition of India.

CHAPTER TWO

Virginity

In turning our attention to the first universal theme which characterizes the Middle East, almost all Westerners are aware of the sharp male-female dichotomy in the area. Some contrast is, of course, quite natural everywhere, as a reflection of the biological differences between the sexes. All cultures distinguish between men and women in terms of roles, status, clothing styles, types of work, etc. However, the Middle East is an extreme case, I believe, and thus it is necessary to explore this distinction as manifest in various aspects of the cultures of the area.

To begin with, there is throughout the Middle East a particular concept of "virginity." Coupled with the concept of "honor," "virginity" guides interpretations of events and channels behavior in a forceful and basic way. The idea of virginity here is not, as it seems to be in European and American circles, restricted to sexual intercourse as such. Rather it is a feeling that no one should give sexual

33

satisfaction of any kind to anyone other than his or her spouse or spouses as the case may be. Sexual stimulation includes not only a flirtatious glance or a caress of the fingers, but even an accidental touching of the body, as the traditional Middle Easterner sees it. Avoidance of violations of "virginity" applies to both men and women. Thus, traditionally, men very frequently are angered when they are placed in a position of being tempted by women by their very presence.

To illustrate, consider the following incident from a story told to me by a young man in Ankara, Turkey. The youth entered a restaurant with a number of male friends. The boys minded their own business, in his words, but a group of girls at a nearby table tried to flirt with them. They ignored the girls for a while but finally had to leave because the girls would not behave themselves. The point here is that the boys felt that they were placed in a very uncomfortable position by having to resist the extremely strong temptation to give sexual satisfaction to the girls, even though the temptation was of a vicarious type that most Westerners would consider completely harmless. These were boys from the rural areas who, while fairly well educated, had been brought up in the country and were thoroughly imbued with traditional morality. They view sex as an uncontrollable drive that they can resist only if they avoid temptation entirely.

A very high percentage of Middle Eastern peasants have ulcerlike stomach symptoms. This struck me as being very odd in 1955 because the life they had led was leisurely and relaxed most of the time. I would have thought that the pace of living would have precluded this type of ailment which is usually associated with stress. However, it seems clear now that this is related to intense psychological stresses caused by the deprivation of certain satisfactions which come from the normal relationships between the sexes, since any relationship is precluded by the culture to prevent the "loss" of virginity.

Problems continually arise between Westernized and traditionally oriented people in the Middle East. For instance, in Syria a man will normally sit between his wife and another man on a bus or in a car to prevent the touching of their bodies which is seen as giving a type of sexual satisfaction and hence is sinful. European-educated Syrians sometimes do not think to sit between their wives and other men. As a result the traditionally oriented Syrian males often become angry because they are placed in a compromising situation.

Westerners tend to view Middle Eastern practices as degrading to women or as a subjugation of them. This is really not the case when the Middle Easterner's beliefs are taken into account. Women are much loved and protected as a rule. This protection is felt to be necessary because the traditional punishment for any lapse in sexual morality, in some cases as small a matter as flirting, was death. Keeping the women segregated and supervised actually makes life much simpler and easier for them because any lapse on their part, be it ever so slight, could result in "intercourse." Not only is the sex urge thought to be an irresistible one, but girls are not taught to be always on guard as are their Western counterparts. Their defenses are external, cultural protections, rather than internal psychological ones. Village men regard women as always willing if they think that they can get away with it, and the men are the protectors of community morality.

In Arabic folktales a mere accusation against a woman was enough to prompt the father or elder brother to kill her, because such an accusation was believed so dire that Allah would punish anyone who made such a charge falsely. Because of the strength of the desire and the extreme penalty for violations, much of Middle Eastern culture has developed around a complex designed to eliminate the possibility of any flirtations or sexual stimulation. Since any slip for the girl is likely to result in irrefutable proof of her digression, especially in the case of pregnancy, the strongest protections have grown up about her, I have been told by Arabs and Turks alike. Actually, it is much easier to seclude the women than the men, particularly in the cities, because of the differences in their activities. With modernization, education and broader range of experience the need for segregation is slowly relaxing, but for the present this is still very important in determining the way Middle Easterners react to certain situations which are unavoidable in a modern society.

Protective devices are utilized in various parts

of the Middle East. In Syria when a man knocks at the door of a city home in the western part of the country, the lady of the house will probably answer him through a small opening in the door. If the master of the house is not at home, the visitor will be asked to come back later. When the husband is home and company arrives, the husband often talks to the visitor outside the house and sends him away without inviting him in. In eastern Syria, however, this would be considered an unforgivable breach of hospitality. In eastern homes there is always a special place for receiving male guests and also a private section of the house wherein no one goes except members of the family, relatives and sometimes a servant. Most city women rarely go outside the confines of this area. In villages, however, and among the tribal peoples on the move, women of necessity must go outside. In such cases they dress in from one to five thicknesses of loose-fitting, flowing garments covered by a large rectangle cloth which gives them the appearance of floating blobs. Since the men and women look much alike, this reduces the possibility of sexual stimulation, except for the flashing eyes. The veil is the shawl-like cloth which covers all but the eyes, and in some areas (e.g., in Pakistan) even the eyes are hidden. The loose-fitting male clothing, also designed to de-sex the human form, is somewhat less extreme than that of the women. The clothing styles are usually thought to be adapted to the climate, but it is my impression that the attempt to disguise the physical features of the body is more important in the

Middle East than the attempt to provide warmth or protection from dust or sun.

Moving from Syria all the way to Morocco, we find here, too, that the house is divided into male and female areas.[1] In the village of Mediouna, some houses have only a single room, but there is always an area, perhaps just a small enclosure in the yard or another small hut, where the women can work without being seen by men who come to visit with the head of the house. Normally the home has two rooms, one in front and one in the back, with the women working in the rear while visitors are entertained in the front. Bedouin tents in northern Syria and Iran are similarly constructed.

In Turkey, homes in some small cities and villages have two living rooms, one to the right of the entrance and one to the left. The one on the right is for entertaining male visitors and the one on the left for women. There is, in addition, a room where food is prepared and other rooms for storage and animals, the degree of elaboration depending on the wealth of the family. Turkish homes, as an alternative pattern, have two rooms, one in front and one in back, with a third built alongside these, a long narrow one with a fireplace on one wall and doors entering into the other two rooms on the opposite wall.[2]

Further manifestations of the desire to keep the sexes apart are to be found in eating practices. In Turkey men eat first. Whether indoors or out, the Turkish village women prepare the food in a special place and a child or young man of the family takes it to the men. Among the Bedouin tribes women are treated with much more equality than they are in many cities, but here too men usually eat in one half of the tent and women prepare the food in the other half.[3] The husband is responsible for securing the food from the kitchen area and passing it on to his guests. The Moghôls of Afghanistan eat in much the same way, "wives and children eating in a separate place. Older boys eat together with the men."[4] In Morocco, "the grown males eat by themselves, served by the women. Women and children eat the leftovers later in seclusion."[5] Such quotes can be found in the literature for many groups in the Middle East, but the wide geographic area covered by the examples given and the fact that nomads and settled village dwellers as well as urbanites are represented, will illustrate how all-pervasive the segregation of the sexes is at mealtime in the Middle East.

The ultimate in seclusion is the practice of *purdah*. Women in *purdah* live most of their adult lives behind walls in a harem area. The word *harem* means only that part of the house to which the women of the household and the master of the house have exclusive access. This practice is disappearing over most of the area, but is still followed by many Iranian, Afghan and Pakistani families. It could probably be found elsewhere in the Middle East, but on a much smaller scale than in this part of Asia. Women who follow this practice are completely covered on the very rare occasions they go onto the streets. One type of Pakistani garb for street wear is all white with a trapdoor completely covering the face. This cloth has a number of tiny holes located before the eyes so that the wearer can see out, but no one can see in. In other areas the clothing may be black or brilliantly colored, with a scarf being wound about the head so as to cover all but the eyes, and in a few areas all but a single eye. Many middle-aged women who have lived this way since childhood would be terrified to go out of their houses in any other clothing though they may be encouraged to do so by their families and the government.

To illustrate the great importance placed upon virginity, we may consider the marriage ceremonies practiced by the peasants in villages of the Middle East. Descriptions of Persian,[6] Turkish,[7] and other[8] weddings are to be found in the literature. The concern here is not so much with the weddings as with their relationship to virginity. Almost everywhere in the Middle East there is at some point in the ceremonies a "test for virginity," or "time of entrance," as it is sometimes called, and if the girl is not a virgin she should be killed by her father or elder brother, according to both Turkish and Arabic informants. Such a killing was reported on the outskirts of Cairo in 1961 in a local newspaper. Great pains are taken to assure that any lack of virginity is not concealed from the husband. Many of the villagers stand about—sometimes someone is designated to watch the act through a hole in the door—the men in the streets and the women on the rooftops. The husband is, by tradition, supposed to come

outside after consummation of the marriage and
signal, often by firing his gun into the air, that the
girl was a virgin. Then two women from the
husband's household hurry in and take out the
sheet, on which the young couple reclined, for
public inspection (usually by just the women), and
Arab women then make a peculiar trilling noise.
This defloration is the climax of the wedding, and a
lack of virginity in the girl would not only cost her
her life, but that of her lover if her family should find
out who he was. To preclude the killing of an
innocent girl, every precaution is taken to insure
that the hymen is not broken by normal activities
before the wedding. But should this occur, the
knowledge is spread throughout the village or tribe.
One can only guess at how often this subterfuge is
used when a case of intercourse has been discovered
before a girl is married. This could be one way out
should a bad situation be discovered.

Weddings in Turkey which I have witnessed
involved village-wide celebrations paid for by the
families of the bride and groom. Bands played
continuously, large quantities of food were eaten,
and the women cooked and gossiped while the men
relaxed, told stories and danced. The celebration
was climaxed in one case when the bride was
brought by her father to her new home. On her trip
between the two houses she was completely covered
with a large sheet so that she appeared as a bright
red, conical tent riding on a horse. The horse is a
symbol of prestige ridden by women only on this
occasion. When the bride arrived at her new home,

the bridegroom climbed onto the roof and dropped a small package of food to her. The girl entered the house and stayed there alone while the groom went off with the men for one last celebration. This bachelor party may consist of dancing, singing and story-telling, or belly-dancers may provide entertainment if the families can afford it. Later the groom will return to consummate the marriage by the "test for virginity." Some Persian weddings are almost identical,[9] even to the pink (Turkish red) dresses. In Morocco one sees essentially the same ceremony.[10]

To understand the significance of these weddings one must realize that this is not the simple uniting of two people as it frequently is in the West, but is a part of a complex struggle for prestige. In the Middle East the extended family, i.e., a line of males including an elderly man, his sons and unmarried daughters, their sons and unmarried daughters, etc., with the women who have married into the family, is the important institutional unit. The marriage of two young people is the responsibility of the heads of the families, and marriages are arranged to bring as much honor to the group as possible. A father tries to marry his children into affluent households. The elaborate and extensive celebration in which the two families feed and entertain the community and sometimes large numbers of guests from neighboring villages, for a protracted period of time, is an occasion to demonstrate their wealth and thereby gain honor. It usually takes the head of the family years to pay off

the debts of a single wedding, and there are usually
several children, but this expense is believed worth-
while when it brings prestige to the families. The
importance of weddings in the life of Middle
Easterners is shown by this statement from an
Iranian bride. "For seven years after a young man
marries, his life will belong to the moneylenders.
But who wants a poor wedding?"[11] On two occasions I have loaned over 300 Turkish lira to a
village family, and I know that this family borrowed
from everyone who would lend them money. The
total cost for the family was approximately 7,000
Turkish lira, and the groom's family spent an equal
amount. Converted into dollars (about $1,600) this
may not sound like much, but to the Turks it is a
tremendous investment. The person to whom we
lent this money was a widow with two daughters,
and the wedding was for her second daughter. In
the village, a lira would buy four loaves of bread
(in 1956), 12 lira would rent a house for a month,
and the lady earned 17 lira a day as a domestic in
Ankara, seven of which she paid for daily transportation. Thus she would have to work approximately
700 days to pay for her daughter's wedding. She
received some help from other members of her
family, but when their children married she would
have to help pay for their weddings. In interviews
with the residents of another village, much farther
from Ankara, the peasants said that weddings in
their village cost between 5,000 and 12,000 lira per
family, depending on the length of the celebration.
These figures in Turkey are about the same as those

for other countries in the Middle East. This expense, however, is not only willingly accepted, but all the money obtainable is poured into the celebrations for each child. Younger children have to postpone their weddings until the earlier debts are paid. No other event in the life of the average peasant will cost as much as this ceremony, and the high point in the wedding is the "test for virginity."

The virginity concept is not restricted to intercourse, but includes any sexual stimulation, yet so far all of the evidence presented has been concerned with intercourse. This was done to show the importance of virginity in the Middle East. Other offenses related to sex can, however, lead to death, at least in theory, for the man as well as the woman. Fulinain (a pseudonym) relates a story of a Marsh Arab who sought the protection of a certain sheik. While under his protection, one of the sheik's sons was caught kissing the refugee's daughter. The girl's father fled with his family because of the disgrace, not only to his daughter but perhaps even more to the honor of the host, but the host killed his own son and had his head delivered to the girl's father to erase the disgrace for the two families. It was not made clear just what happened to the girl.[12] The emotional intensity of this act perhaps cannot be grasped without a knowledge of how much these people love their children, and especially their sons. This story may not be true, but the Arabs tell such stories, and insist that they are true, indicating that this is an ideal cultural norm, if not an actual behavioral pattern. It is difficult to even guess how often this sort of thing happens. However, repeated questioning of Turkish and Arabic informants brought out that this was the proper course of action in such a situation, and it was also said that such slayings in the villages were not usually reported to the government.

The broad traditional concept of virginity is still an important moral force in the Middle East. In 1960 one of the female translators in my office in Ankara went in a taxi with me to Ulus to buy a type-writer. We sat as far apart as possible. The girl was a highly educated "modern" Turk in Western cloth-ing. Despite this facade of urbanization, her husband came to the office in a rage because a friend of his had seen the taxi on Ataturk Boulevard and reported the incident to him. This, despite our being in the company of the taxi driver in broad daylight, and on an official errand for our office. The husband insisted that his wife was a "stationary" translator, meaning one who did not go in and out of the office, and that if such a thing happened again he would take appropriate action. I never found out what this action might have been, as I never took that trans-lator out of the office again. Numerous similar incidents could be related. There are many urban Turks and Arabs who have assimilated so much Western culture that it is hard to tell them from educated Westerners, yet they still make many day-to-day judgments on the basis of the traditional values.

The concept of virginity, then, as expressed to me

by Turks and Arabs, is a dynamic force within the culture. There are strong restrictions on male-female cooperative labor, except where a husband-wife team is concerned, segregation of guests on the basis of sex (architectural forms are altered to provide male and female rooms) and the sanctioning of murder, at least theoretically, for as little a matter as a kiss or flirtation.

The virginity of a Middle Eastern girl being lost by a kiss is not understood by Europeans and much of the associated behavior of Middle Easterners appears to them to be irrational. At the Gazi Teacher's Training Institute in Ankara, one of my best students was caught on a balcony with a boy, and it was rumored that they had kissed, though there was no evidence this had happened. The administration wanted to expel the girl, but through the insistence of the American teachers she was allowed to remain in school. None of the Americans understood the depth of feeling regarding this incident. To us, nothing had happened, but in the eyes of the Gazi staff the girl had compromised her virginity. The non-Turkish instructors unanimously felt that what had happened had nothing to do with the girl's ability to become a good English teacher.

All cultures have moral codes and any deviation from the code leads to the belief that these people are likely to be a bad influence on the younger generations on the assumption that they will probably violate other cultural norms. In many American colleges a girl caught in the act of intercourse probably would be expelled, regardless of her academic promise. The values of Western culture are often as non-rational as those of the Middle East.

Conflicts and differences of the type described above are far more significant than some of the more obvious physical ones. These subtle differences are not only not understood, but Westerners are not even aware that there is a problem. It is my belief that a careful study of the cultures of the "developing" nations in which American AID groups are working could make the American effort infinitely more effective. This would eliminate a considerable amount of tension and international misunderstanding. The examples were drawn mostly from my personal experience in Turkey partly because they are personal and hence more meaningful to me, but also because very little of this type of information is presented in the available literature on the Middle East, and a demonstration of the force of these themes or patterns in daily life can be documented only by describing observable behavior.

CHAPTER THREE

Honor

Every human being wishes to be respected by the members of his social group. The quest for honor and prestige is certainly one of the most important motivations in the lives of Middle Easterners, whether they live in a city or village, or belong to a nomadic group. Loss of respect is a terrible emotional trauma to a person in the Middle East, so much so that he will go to almost any extreme to preserve his "honor." To understand this we need to look briefly at the complex behavior patterns which bring "respect" to a Middle Easterner, and then examine the way they influence the day-to-day decisions he makes.

We should note that every action of a man, woman or child in Middle-Eastern society is a matter of honor or dishonor not only to himself but to his entire family. An individual is nothing, except as part of a larger group. The size of this group as well as its exact composition varies greatly from place to place, but almost always it includes a man's mother, father, male siblings and his male children. The concern over the loss of virginity is not so much a matter of individual disgrace, but one of loss of respect for all who belong to the group of the offender. If the individual were the only one concerned there would be no need for others to intervene. But loss of virginity is perhaps the most serious thing that can befall an individual, as the Middle Easterner sees it, therefore the penalties are the most severe. The penalty for loss of virginity for a female is death, but the penalty is not always enforced. This is an ideal difficult for Westerners to understand. The reactions of members of a cultural group are not abstract concepts but are those of people caught in the throes of severe emotional stress. Their course in a given situation depends on these conflicting emotions and drives. Therefore, different people in identical situations will not do identical things despite the cultural norms. Consider the feelings of the person who must carry out this dreadful punishment, the father or brother. It is no wonder then that the penalty is not always enforced. I have been told that in the desert there are small local groups which have no "honor." These groups are composed of families which have sacrificed their honor. This could happen if a girl were loved so greatly by her family that her father and brothers could not kill her when her transgression was discovered. To protect her life, they sacrificed their honor and fled the group to which they had belonged, because if they hadn't, a more distant relative, one not so strongly attached to the guilty party, such as a father's brother, would have killed her. Any stain on the blood line is remembered for generations and children from those families are not wanted in marriage by "good" families.

In cases of proven adultery, i.e., where the girl proves not to be a virgin on her wedding night, she rarely escapes death, but where there is doubt, there is enough flexibility in the system for the man who might hate his sister to get rid of her and for the one who loves her to escape the fateful job, at least until there is irrefutable proof. Then he must act or the entire family will suffer a terrible disgrace; if the father or brothers are unable to kill her, someone else will.

To illustrate the deep fear of the loss of honor, consider the story told by an old Marsh Arab and published by Fulinain:[1]

In an argument a man claims that the sister of his antagonist is "dishonoring" the tribe in her relationship with a man. The man goes home, says to his sister, "the price of adultery is death," and stabs the girl to death, despite his presumed great love for her. The story may not be true, but the truth or falsity is not important, as the story is told to illustrate how young men should act, and clearly reflects a cultural value. I have heard similar stories from Arabs and have been told by Turks that this would be the most honorable course to follow.

Najafi[2] tells of a Persian wedding in which the bride backed out at the last moment because she knew she was not a virgin. People wondered why she did not go through with the wedding. The

father disowned the girl and had her arrested because of the dishonor she had cast on his house. She
was subsequently released, due to the intercession of
Najafi herself, and disappeared from the village
because someone would have killed her had she not.

In Afghanistan adultery is reportedly punished
by "immediate killing by the aggrieved husband, or
by stoning to death. Punishment for unmarried
adulterers was . . . whipping which might or might
not result in death."[3] In Iraq, Dorothy Van Ess
says that she was greatly shaken when the first
"honor" killing occurred.[4] She states that a father
had killed a young girl because she had committed
adultery—or at least she had been accused of it so
publicly that he could not ignore the charge—and
the murder was necessary to wash away the disgrace. Mrs. Van Ess further writes that another
woman became ineligible for marriage because it
was rumored she had sent notes to a young man,[5]
and an Arab woman is quoted as saying, ". . .
sooner or later everyone dies. What matters is one's
honor."[6] Such examples abound in the literature,
and at this point we are not concerned about the
validity of the reports, but rather with the "stains
on one's honor" which are regarded as so important
to people in the Middle East that they will kill those
dear to them rather than be disgraced. These
stories are bound to have a profound influence upon
a Middle Easterner's code of adult conduct.

The act of killing a guilty party is not just to
preclude a recurrence of the sin, but rather is a way
of washing the stain from the family honor. Fre-

quently in cases of adultery the man and woman are both killed if the man is known, because he has contributed to the dishonor. One factor which protects a man in this situation would be uncertainty about his guilt combined with the fear of a blood feud. If a man kills a youth who is supposed to have violated his sister, and the young man is innocent, or if his family believes that he is innocent, the relatives of the youth will then have to avenge his death. This can start a chain reaction resulting in a long series of murders. Thus unless there is no doubt as to who the offender is, no action is likely to be taken.

The honor of a group can also be soiled by outsiders. Once more Mrs. Van Ess's book provides a good illustration. A young, well-educated man in Iraq married a girl considered to be of a higher class. A sheik from the girl's tribe entered the husband's office in Bagdad one day and killed him. The sheik was sentenced to death at first, but then the sentence was commuted and he actually served only two and a half years for the crime. He was later hailed as a hero by his own people when he returned to the tribal camp for having erased the stain resulting from a member of his group marrying beneath her station.[7] The blame for loss of honor was placed on the man because he should have known better than to involve himself with a member of an honored family. The real pity in this particular case was that both partners in the marriage were Western educated and believed that the thinking had become more enlightened.

Barth reports that Kurdish tribes in Iraq do not follow the classic type of "blood feud"[8] wherein, if someone in a particular lineage is murdered, the members of that lineage are honor-bound to kill a member of the murderer's lineage of approximately the same sex, age and rank. However, a Bedouin friend of mine who lived for over two years in a Kurdish area on the Syrian-Iraqi border says that the Syrian Kurds do have essentially the same type of blood feuds as the Bedouin. This means that if a man is murdered, his brothers and their sons are responsible for the killing of someone in the family of the murderer. If the brothers fail to take appropriate action, then more remote kinsmen will. The man to be killed in retaliation need not be the one who did the original killing, but should be of equal rank with the victim. These feuds sometimes continue until they involve whole federations of many tribal groups, and they so disrupt the area that other groups initiate procedures for "digging and burying," which means balancing things off. This "digging and burying" is done in the home of a neutral sheik. The leaders of the feuding factions list their casualties, marking off man for man and rank for rank until all the dead are accounted for. If it comes out even, the feud is over. If uneven, the side with the fewer casualties pays a "blood price," usually a combination of money and animals, to the side with the greater losses. The only such feud involving large groups that my Bedouin friend had witnessed took place in the early thirties between two very large Bedouin confederations. This indicates that major feuds have been rare, even among the Arabs, in recent years. Stories of blood feuds are common throughout the Middle East, and the type of vengeance necessary, i.e., the death of someone from the murderer's kin group (usually patri-lineage), clearly indicates that it is usually the punishment of the group which is sought rather than the punishment of the individual.

Along with the general concept of "honor" is the responsibility to offer protection to anyone seeking it. Fulinain provides an interesting description of the institution of "protection" during a blood feud.[9] A man can demand protection for himself, and sometimes for his family, from anyone except a member of the group against which he is feuding. A Middle Easterner is honor-bound to give this pro-tection, but if the man should be murdered, even by a member of the tribe against which he is feuding, while so "protected," the tribe of the pro-tector must feud with that of the murderer to avenge the disgrace. Failure to respond to an appeal for protection results in serious loss of honor. In Fulinain's story the protection was granted but a fight ensued and the tribe of the protector was defeated by the larger tribe of the murderer. Ap-parently, however, the stain was washed away by the fighting even though the protectors lost and many of their tribe were killed. Many from the winning tribe must also have been killed, and this demonstrated to other tribes that the protector's group could be depended upon to fight and thus were honorable men.

Another description of protection, this for the Riffian tribes in Morocco, is found in Coon's *Caravan*.[10] A Riffian clan was besieged by its neighbors. The group under attack sent a messenger who sacrificed a goat on the sill of the mosque so that blood was splattered on the door, a symbolic request for protection. This was a "shame compulsion which no man of honor could refuse."[11] The important point here is that there would be no punishment for a group who refused the plea for help (protection) except loss of respect. Yet again and again we find in the literature statements to the effect that no man of honor could or would refuse these pleas even though the consequences are almost always dire.

The Kabyles of Algeria are reported to know "no other code than honor."[12] The crimes of murder and adultery[13] are listed together as if roughly equivalent in value. The penalties for murder and adultery are not spelled out, but common practice in the area calls for the death of a member of the guilty party's lineage, as described in the case of blood feuds. Of the Shawia, it is reported that "a group . . . acts with vigor when its 'honor' is compromised by adultery. . . ."[14] The husband can either repudiate a wife or put her to death, but the family puts pressure on him to assure a "proper vengeance," which is usually death.

The literature leads one to believe that of the three offenses, murder, insult and adultery, insult provokes the most violent reaction. Actually, adultery is regarded as a kind of insult or disgrace.

Perhaps even murder is an indication that the members of the murderer's group have so little respect for the other group that they do not fear to kill one of its members.

Respect is closely linked to the concept of "honor," and the outward manifestations of the respect complex in the Middle East are best interpreted as a type of fear that is quite different from the Western concept of "honor." Several times when I played with my son in Turkey, I was told to be more distant and severe because if I weren't he wouldn't respect me.

Turning to the international situation, I found that Middle Easterners respect nations which demonstrate the power and ability to defeat their enemies, concluding that it would be profitable to join with such a powerful ally. Never in my personal dealings with people in the area did I hear anyone comment on the justness of the large powers in the struggle for prestige. The highest point of United States prestige was when American troops landed in Lebanon in 1958. Westerners have a tendency to think that the people of the area might feel that we were interfering with the internal policies of an independent country and think less of us. I am speaking here of the reactions of the common man, not the official position taken by the government of the United Arab Republic. It must be remembered that the average Middle Easterner looks upon his government as an "enemy." Centuries of exploitation by the central authorities are responsible for this feeling. Many leaders are Western educated and while they do not accept many of the values of the West, they understand it. Many published positions which emanate from Cairo are designed to make Americans, in particular, feel guilty in order to get us to cease and desist. Often these reflect the Arab's very astute awareness of how to handle powers beyond his control rather than an honest statement of policy. The United States was generally admired and respected almost everywhere by the man in the street because it had the force, and used it, to carry out its wishes. We will return to this in more detail later when the power structure of the Middle East is discussed.

The highest kind of respect in the Middle East is gained from exploits on the field of battle, not by being just or kindly. Old men are respected and feared because they know how to defeat younger and stronger opponents, not because they are kindly old grandfathers in the Western ideal. Youngsters are not taught to respect a man because he is honest, hard working, etc., but because he is old and/or powerful. This is not meant to disparage the Middle Eastern concept of respect but to point out the difference between their concept and that of the West so that both sides can better deal with each other.

I am reminded of something that happened in a certain country in the Middle East. A government official was accused of taking money from his government. He was tried, found guilty and sentenced to five years in prison. Later it was found that he was not guilty, but when his family at-

tempted to have him released they were unsuccess-
ful, because publicizing the government's mistake
would have reduced the people's respect for the
government. The man was left in prison for the full
five-year term. Subsequently he killed himself because of the loss of honor to his family. The American ideal would require that the government
restore the man to his proper place in society as well
as make some restitution for his imprisonment. The
ideal is not always achieved in either society, but I
wish only to point out the difference in viewpoints.

I have asserted that fear of loss of honor (or shame
if one prefers) was an extremely strong drive in
Middle Eastern cultures, and that certain actions
could loosely be labeled as insults, resulting in
rather severe consequences. It was further asserted
that an individual was nothing except as a member
of a group. It is probably best to treat most statements about the Middle East as hypotheses.

To illustrate a type of group referred to loosely as
families or lineages, consider an Anatolian (Turkish)
village. The smallest unit in the particular village
studied, and the most cohesive, was a patrilineal
extended family. This consists of an old man, who
was the head of the family, with his wife or wives,[15]
his sons with their wives, and his unmarried daughters as well as grandsons, great grandsons, etc., with
their wives and unmarried sisters. This unit is under
the complete control of the old man whose strongest
whips are the threat of disinheritance and the power
to call curses down on the disobedient. These are
much more potent threats than most Americans

would imagine because the villager without land has, in most cases, no way to support himself except to beg. Further, since most peasants, until very recently, looked with horror on the idea of leaving the village, the threat of disinheritance is a powerful club for enforcing obedience. The fear of curses is very real in an almost totally illiterate population which looks on all illness either as a curse, witchcraft, or punishment for sin sent from God. Marriages are arranged by the family, usually the father, and it is his responsibility to come up with the dowry. Refusal or inability to put up a sufficient amount of goods and money could result in a poor marriage for either boy or girl, and no one wants a cheap wedding. These threats forced a high degree of conformity with the wishes of the patriarch. This family unit usually lived in one house until the sons were 32 to 50 years old, unless the family head died. The eldest son usually kept the family home and his brothers built houses of their own. Thus new extended families came into existence, and the families of brothers cooperated under the direction of the eldest for some time after the break-up of the original family. These ties, however, were much looser after the death of the father. As long as the father lived, every member was responsible for the welfare of the entire family and also responsible to it for his or her every action. This feeling, even among Western-educated city-dwellers, is still very strong. In Ankara I knew an engineer, trained at an American university and married to an American girl. When faced with an important decision, he would frequently fly to Istanbul and ask his father and older brother what he should do. This tradition is much stronger in the villages than in Ankara.

Among the Bedouin in northern Syria a similar situation exists, except that the family break-up takes place as the father builds homes for each of his sons. This is done in order of age whenever the father has enough money and feels that the sons are ready to leave or when the homestead gets too crowded. The city of Raqqa is the winter quarters for several tribes, many of which have permanent houses for their extended families in town, but when on the move each family unit (father, mother and children) has its own tent. The tents of the heads of households differ from those of the sons by being larger and in having a section always ready for the entertainment of guests. A similar system appears to be operative among the Kurdish tribes of Iraq, as illustrated by the Barth quote, "if a father can afford the necessary expense in tents and utensils, he will set up an independent household for his married son. Poor people. . . may find this impossible."[16] Barth explains further, "a man can expect political support . . . primarily (from) brothers, sons, and brothers' sons."[17] Thus the details of the arrangements differ somewhat from place to place but basically these units are composed of a man, his sons and their sons with wives and unmarried daughters. In Algeria, the Shawia obey the grandfather who "has complete authority over his children and grandchildren, who live under the same roof or in contiguous dwellings. . . . The extended family of the patriarchal type is the fundamental social unit."[18] This seems to be very similar in other Algerian groups. In the case of the Kabyles, "the extended family . . . brings together . . . descendants from a common male . . . uniting several generations."[19] This system also exists among the Moghôls of Afghanistan, for ". . . not only is the land owned and operated jointly, but brothers live in immediate proximity to one another and during the summer live in the same Khail."[20] Among the Marsh Arabs of Iraq, one of the most divergent groups in the Middle East, the basic unit in terms of responsibility for crimes is the Khowwan, or group of brothers. This group is found "habitually acting as a single unit . . . in paying compensation for certain crimes. They may be sons of one father, or they may have a common grandfather."[21] It was customary to demand payment for certain wrongs in women. "The wronged party has the right to choose any woman or women from the culprit's group responsible for payment."[22] This group very closely parallels the extended families described for other cultures in the preceding paragraphs, and the responsibility of the group for crimes is quite clear.

Throughout the literature the implication is that the welfare of the individual is far less important than that of the group. This was illustrated for Arab, Turk, Kurd and Moghôl groups over an area ranging from Afghanistan to Algeria to emphasize that the practice was not limited to villages, cities, tribes or specific ethnic groups or localities.

The sample of Middle Eastern cultures we have used is actually inadequate for making such generalizations, but it is highly probable that this pattern of family solidarity will be found in the great majority of Middle Eastern communities. In Turkey for example two villages five miles apart can be radically different, one endogamous and the other exogamous. Any assumption that neighboring tribes or villages are very similar obviously would not hold up. Many conquerors have dominated the Middle East thoughout the past 6,000 years, each leaving his imprint, but each affecting different groups in different ways. Even for "well-known" groups our data on cultural variation is limited. We have a good deal of literature on the Bedouin, for example, but even here there are wide and undefined differences from one "tribe" to another. Many Bedouin groups, i.e., Arabi ud-Dar (house Arabs) as defined by Coon,[23] consider themselves to be true Bedouin because many stay around the city in tents rather than houses. Some summer in the city while others winter there, and there are, according to one native informant, great differences in the way the various groups live. Here I am only trying to present generalizations which appear to be true based upon available data.

Returning to the subject of adultery by the women of the family, this is one of the most prevalent topics among men in the coffee houses and in oral literature. Others include harm to someone under the protection of particular families or tribes, improper marriages and failure to give protection when it is asked. Many things are much less serious than these, however. I know of one case in 1960 in which an Ankara University coed committed suicide because she had failed an examination. This she thought would bring disgrace to her family. There are undoubtedly a great many additional types of dishonor, few of which have been thoroughly explored even for a single culture. If two families in one village are at odds, settling the dispute is left to them unless the security of the larger group is threatened. Family quarrels will then be put aside to defend the tribe against outside attack and taken up again when the external threat is gone. However, it should be noted that the insult is felt more strongly the closer the relationship of the family member to the injured party.

So far family solidarity has been emphasized and it appears almost as if the individual were completely subjugated by the family. But there are important compensations for the individual, especially when he is attempting to foster his own family's welfare. Many times when a new job was created by some joint action of the American and Turkish governments, close friends would approach me to hire one of their relatives. Usually this person was unqualified for the position, and the reaction of the average American worker was that these people were dishonest or immoral. In many cases when I worked with Turks they unashamedly (in fact proudly) hired their relatives. The critical point here is that it would be dishonorable for a traditionally oriented Middle Easterner to do otherwise. He is honor-bound by all that he holds sacred to promote the welfare of his extended family group.

It is as wrong for a Middle Easterner to tell about the faults of his relatives as it is for an American to create faults in his colleagues to secure personal advantage. The acceptance of Western values would force a Middle Easterner to be dishonorable in the eyes of his family and friends, and following the traditions of the Middle East forces him to be dishonorable in the eyes of Americans. Is it any wonder then that the government officials attempting to Westernize their countries are rarely understood either by the Westerners or by their own people?

The Western specialist working in the Middle East is frequently misled by the apparent modernity and education of his local counterparts. The Middle Eastern values run deep, having been learned at an early age, so that Western-educated Turks, Arabs or Iranians may appear to be "Westernized," yet in their daily lives they may operate on the basis of a set of subconscious values which are a basic part of their traditional society. They are not being dishonest, but simply human.

CHAPTER FOUR

Power Structure

One of the great mysteries about the Middle East for Westerners seems to be the instability of governments. One would expect that this instability would have its roots in the traditional power structure because people tend to react in terms of unconscious value systems, which change very slowly. Thus a study of the power structure of tribes, villages and small cities should provide some insight into this problem.

Returning to Coon's description of the Middle Eastern cultures as a mosaic, we see an area populated mostly by villagers who did not do much fighting. Rather they preferred to pay tribute to nomadic tribes for their protection because most of their time was required to care for their crops.[1] The nomad who did not till the soil, had, on the other hand, a great deal more time during which he could indulge in non-productive activities such as feuding with other groups, raiding, etc. Therefore, it was among the nomads that a proud code of military

65

conduct evolved. This was basically a code of individual honor, not one governing opposing armies. Warfare was a game through which one gained power and prestige, but was not the scourge of mankind it is today because the technology necessary for killing large numbers of people was not highly developed.

Superimposed on the power structures of the villages and nomads are the cities. These large urban centers began to develop in the Middle East many centuries before Christ and have been a significant factor in the power struggle ever since. Cities have an advantage over villages and nomadic tribal groups in that they can muster and train large, well-equipped armies. Thus a city could easily subjugate any individual nomadic group as well as any single village. Possibly in response to this threat the tribes formed confederations to enable them to amass enough warriors to challenge the cities. Their greatest protection, however, lay in their mobility and the vast expanse of desert over which it was difficult for large armies to move. Cities could, of course, combine their armies in response to tribal confederations, but the nomads would then break up into small, self-sufficient groups and disappear into the hills. The cities were dependent on food secured either by purchase or tribute from their subject peoples. Caravans had to transport the supplies from outlying areas, and these caravans were vulnerable to hit-and-run attacks by roving bands. Maintaining the large professional armies of the cities became a major problem if the nomadic peoples kept moving, and if the villagers hid, their crops or their supplies were taken by raiding nomads.

The brute strength of a central authority has never been sufficient to effectively subjugate an entire region, and what subjugation there was had to be tempered with tact and diplomacy. Centralized authority has been generally equated with taxes and oppression in the minds of the small local groups. Much of the shifting of loyalites from one city to another was an attempt to find which of the oppressors was the least distasteful.

A brief description of the power structure of the area over the past 6,000 years reveals loose confederations of villages, tribes and/or cities, each competing with the other to promote its own best interest. If one became too powerful, the subject tribes would unite and sometimes join a different power group to preserve as much of their autonomy as possible. When the tribes became too powerful, more and more cities would join together, enlisting or conscripting villagers who were perhaps also suffering from tribal raids, to bring the confederations into line. A strong leader would either persuade or force large numbers to follow him and gain control over a substantial region for a time, but these structures were always maintained by force or the threat of force.

These groupings worked on several levels. Pierre Bourdieu gives a very clear description of the relationships back of this type of power arrangement in Algeria.[2] "The family is the alpha and omega of the whole system . . . it is the indissociable [unbreakable] atom of the society."[3] The "family" Bourdieu describes is the patrilineal extended family discussed in the previous chapter. However, while this extended family is the basic unit, Bourdieu says there are larger groupings based on kinship which are also functional in all groups in Algeria. "Everywhere the social system is patterned on the model of the genealogical system . . . permitting . . . dispersed and ramified groups to discover common ancestors."[4] These clan-like units trace descent through a line of males to a common ancestor, sometimes fictional, who is often worshipped. The clan is said to be a very stable unit, though from the individual's point of view less so than the extended family. Above the clan there is the village or local camp group, either of which may contain several clans, and there appears to be an almost infinite variety of groupings possible, depending on the reason for subdividing. The entire tribe (all people who are thought to be Kabylia, etc.) is considered by the people to have originally been a single family and all subdivisions are the result of the breaking up of this family. "Each brother is a potential breaking point. . . ."[5] This is an *a posteriori* rationalization,[6] but it illustrates the belief of the group in kinship ties as well as in realignments, when the power struggle indicates that realignments are advantageous to a sub-group or individual capable of making a change.

Bourdieu diagrams the power arrangement as a number of concentric squares with the relationships existing between two people being stronger if they belong to the same square and weaker if they belong to different squares.[7] To illustrate this point, let us say that two individuals are embroiled in a dispute. Usually they will settle the argument peacefully. If this is not possible, and violence erupts, the brothers will take sides; if the two combatants belong to the same extended family, and when the problem becomes acute, the family head will step in and solve it for them. If they belong to different family groups, it becomes a quarrel between the two families. If this erupts into violence, then the clan chiefs are called upon to resolve it, possibly with the aid of the council.

If there are four clans in one village or camp group, and the disputants belong to different clans, it becomes a quarrel between the two clans, and the village council may have to settle it, especially if the other clans take sides and become involved in active fighting. When these disputes occur Bourdieu indicates (see notes 3, 4, 5 and 6) that families change clans and then later rationalize the move. This system as it operates in Algeria appears to be much more rigid than that of many societies described in the literature, but even here there is some flexibility. This system is, according to Bourdieu, the same for the Kabyles, Shawia, Mozabites and Arabic-speaking peoples. The above list of cultural or ethnic groups includes Arab and Berber as well as sedentary and nomadic groups in Algeria.

In Afghanistan, Schurman says that "the over-whelming majority of the population considers itself and is considered to be a member of some ethnic group: Afghan, Uzbek, Hazara, etc. . . . People are generally aware of the fact that they are members of some large common descent group . . . they are (also) members of a small, largely local common descent group. . . . However, most informants were not aware of the descent relationships between the small and the larger groups, and information on that subject was usually confused."[8] This "confusion" could be the result of the natural instability of the larger groupings rather than simply the vestige of an older and perhaps stronger organization, as Schurman suggests, though it may be a result of both. Nine tribal names are given for different Moghôl groups and "when asked about groups within the Marda [one of the tribal groups] informants merely referred to different villages. Even in this respect, because of the lack of stability in settlement, none of the Moghôls conceived of themselves as tied to a given region."[9] The "lack of stability" indicates that the families felt more or less free from alignment with a particular group unless it suited their purposes to remain aligned. However, the villages throughout the Middle East do seem to be much more stable. People move to other villages less quickly than nomadic camp groups shift their allegiance from one group to another or form new groups. One can always take his tent and move a short distance away from an antagonist in a nomadic camp, but in a small peasant community this is difficult. Hence villagers are less likely to quarrel openly.

To return to the power structure in Afghanistan, the tribes are further subdivided into two sections, which may be descent groups (perhaps fictional as in Algeria) or they may be some sort of moiety. Schurman suggests that these are remnants of a larger number of descent groups. On the basis of what we know about social organization generally in the Middle East it would appear that these may be the remnants of old confederations which have been destroyed by pressures from the central governments or internal stresses. Once again, the feeling of the natives for descent alignments makes them rationalize the groups in kinship terms. These larger groupings, below or within the tribe, which are usually called clans, exhibit all sorts of characteristics which are certainly atypical for clans.

The over-all appearance of these clanlike units fits the picture for the traditional clan fairly well until one begins to look into the functioning within the culture. Clans are as a rule very rigid organizations, which trace their descent from common ancestors. The description of the Khail in Afghanistan[10] indicates clearly the lack of rigid groupings above the extended family for the Moghôl groups described. The general picture presented by Schurman for Afghanistan seems to be like that in Algeria, despite the distance between the two places and the realization that in one region we are looking at Moghôl groups and in the other at Berber and Arab.

The Basseri of southern Persia are very clearly described by Barth.[11] He mentions that in the past

the Basseri were members of the Khamseh confederacy; but "this grouping has today lost most
of its political and social meaning."[12] The author
describes the society as being composed of household
units; each contains a family nucleus and in each
everything is owned and controlled by the head of
the household.[13] Only one of these "families" in one
group consisting of 32 tents was an extended family
of the type already discussed. However, the camp
group is "in a very real sense the primary community of nomadic Basseri society . . . their re-
lations . . . are relatively constant, while other
contacts are passing. . . ."[14] The basic unit of
solidarity is the family and the head of each such
group can take his family and disassociate it from
the camp at any time. Every day, according to
Barth, decisions must be made on which there must
be unanimous agreement. Anyone who disagrees
can simply stay by himself, but if he does he loses
the protection of the group as well as the emotional
satisfactions derived from association with close
relatives, so important throughout the Middle East.
However, each camp group has a leader, and
Barth's description of the way this group is held
together coincides almost perfectly with a description given me by an Arab Bedouin, so that it
would appear that the nomadic groups of this
entire region, whether Arab, Kurd or Persian-
speaking, have a common power structure. One of
the strongest cohesive forces appears to be the
natural suspicion felt toward all non-group persons
and a degree of trust for all the members of the

group which is directly proportional to the closeness of the relationship. You trust a brother much more than you trust a third cousin, but both are trusted more than an outsider.

Bourdieu diagrammed the power structure as a series of concentric squares, but I will use the graphic device of a series of circles to illustrate the same thing (see p. 74). If two individuals are in the same circle they trust each other more than if one is in a different circle on any level of social organization. If the largest circle represents the ethnic group as a whole, the one below that a tribe, the next smaller a section and so forth down to the smallest circle which represents the extended family, there is great trust between members of the smallest circles, quite a bit in those of the next higher circle, a little in the larger circles but none in people outside the largest circle. The larger circles are important mainly in case of a quarrel between an in-group member and anyone outside the largest circle. Every member of the society within the circle is honor bound to defend any other member.

A very conservative factor in all aspects of Middle Eastern life is the tendency, which can also be observed from Morocco to Afghanistan, to make a change only by unanimous consent. Since getting everyone in any group to agree on anything new is very difficult, even relatively minor changes in routine become serious problems, and major in-novations almost impossible. Every morning, Barth says, there is the decision as to whether one should move on. This sets up the possibility of a split in

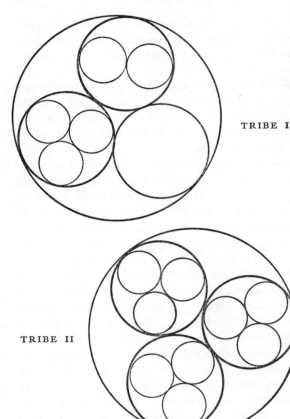

TRIBE I

TRIBE II

This diagram shows the hierarchy of loyalties of the Middle Easterners as well as the traditional power structure. Individuals within any circle are more loyal to each other than to people not included in that circle, and the loyalties are more cohesive within the smaller circles than in the larger ones.

the camp group. Therefore, the leader must be fairly skillful in dealing with the heads of households in order to get them to agree with what he feels the group must do. Leadership generally follows a particular male line, but this is true only as long as the man is able to consolidate his own following and keep any factions from uniting against him. The second factor in effective leadership of a nomadic camp is the manipulation of kinship ties. In a crisis relatives can be relied on generally to respond with support for the leader, hence one wants to arrange marriages, etc., so as to create as many relatives as possible.

Moving from Persia to Afghanistan, the small endogamous groups studied by Schurman form a web of interlocking kinship ties because matrilineal descent is reckoned and one owes loyalty to affinal as well as consanguinal relatives.[15] This is, according to the literature and my own experience, unusual in the Middle East. One normally owes loyalty only to the male line; females are more or less lost to the family when they are married off, and females who come into the family do not usually bind a man to support their relatives.

The camp group is said to be roughly equivalent to a village in terms of its functioning, as these two types of groups are the smallest units in size which are economically self-sufficient. The camp group may break up, just as peasants may leave their home village, but distrust of outsiders, kinship ties and emotional satisfactions inherent in the day-to-day contacts with close friends and relatives tend to hold the group together, while the independence of each household head and natural conflicts generated by the routine of daily living and working together tend to pull it apart. These two opposing forces are constantly at work, and running a camp group (or for that matter any group) in the Middle East depends on the ability of the leader to cajole, threaten and argue his cause better than anyone else.

Each camp is made up of one or more herding units which will separate when pasturage is short, but usually they graze in close proximity unless something occurs to divide them, such as a major disagreement between heads of households. At such a time one or two herding units may break away from the camp group and form a new unit. Villages are more stable because a break involves locating a water supply sufficient to sustain a colony and establishing a new village which may fight over the land needed either with the parent group, if they attempt to settle too close, or an alien group if they move too far away.

All Basseri consider themselves to be members of a single tribe with a paramount chief. The tribe in turn consists of twelve *tira* (descent groups), each of which is further divided into sections which are composed of *oulads*. The power of the chief goes from tribe to section to *oulad* then directly to the head of a household. Thus the camp group has no official recognition in the formalized power structure despite its fundamental role in the society. Barth's discussion[16] makes it quite clear that the Basseri present the same problems, when one attempts to

understand their power structure, as do the groups
discussed earlier. The genealogies collected did not
correlate with the actual organization of the sub-
tribal groups; " . . . thus the Ahl-e-Gholi are
supposed to be derived from the Qarachai Qashqai,
the Salvestani from the village of Sarvestan and the
Ahli Shah Gholi and possibly the Hanai from the
Arabs. Groups carrying the same names and identified as collateral are also found in different tribes."[17]
This quote indicates clearly what was stated by
Bourdieu for the Algerian groups and postulated for
the Moghôls, i.e., the larger descent groups break
up and join with other groups not related when it is
to their advantage to do so. It seems that both Barth
and Schurman were looking too hard for kinship
ties within these groups. While kinship ties are
important in terms of close relatives, it would appear
that they are hardly noted beyond the patrilineal
extended families, but since close kinship is so important and relatives have a tendency to be trusted
more than non-relatives, larger groupings tend
generally to have related groups in them. However,
there do not appear to be any real formalized clan
structures, but rather simply large groups which are
rationalized on kinship logic because the people,
seeing the majority of their group vaguely related,
assume that there must be some sort of lineage
principle operating. They in turn mislead the field
investigator who is looking for kinship ties in the
first place. I see no other way to explain Barth's
statements about his frustrations because the Basseri
were, "unable to expand them [lists of relatives]

into ramifying genealogies of the whole *oulad*. . . . When asked to designate the main segments of an *oulad*, different informants would give widely different pictures. . . . The pedigrees I collected also show a surprising lack of fit with the formalized pattern of grouping into *oulad* and section."[18] Thus Barth's statements clearly show that the groups above the camp, even the tribe or ethnic unit, appear to be composed of groups related to other groups which are Arabs, are in the Qashqai confederacy and in one case are part of a village. This is not a confused picture as I see it, but a reflection of the brittle nature of all groups above the family, family being defined slightly differently in each case. Larger groups fragment and sometimes a small number of families, a camp group, a grazing unit or perhaps an entire *oulad* or section, may even leave the tribe and join another because of conflict of interest within the unit. The groups headed by brothers are by far the most stable units and disintegration of such groups is rare.

It seems clear that the Basseri of Iraq, Moghôl groups of Afghanistan, Bedouin of Syria, as well as the different types of cultures in Algeria for which we have any appreciable data have a very similar power structure, and Bourdieu's graphic representation of it as a system of concentric squares provides us with an excellent vehicle for understanding the instability of units on all levels above the family in the Middle East.

To review the power structure briefly: in the smallest square is the patriarchal type of family, usually a father, sons, grandsons, etc., with their spouses and unmarried sisters. However, in some cultures only a part of this complete patrilineal extended family is found in the inner square. Within this lowest unit there is rarely any fragmentation until after the death of the father because of joint concern for the inheritance as well as the general fear that the old man can call down curses on disobedient children. Quarrels within this group are quickly settled by the patriarch. Above this unit, division is possible on five or six levels, and the groups in a dispute are determined by the group membership of the participants. The cohesiveness of the group is inversely proportional to its size; the smaller the group the less likely is it to split up. This appears to apply more to nomadic groups than to settled populations, but it also seems true for confederations of villages and cities. Each group is responsible for contributing economically to the support of the next higher level, and this payment is usually resented because in some instances it is as much as half of one's total production. If by changing groups one can reduce these payments there would be at least some motivation to shift loyalties. Also one pays partially for the protection that the larger group offers, and if another group offers better protection, especially at a lower price, a group is likely to change its affiliation.

This traditional power structure gives some insight into current instability because rigid national boundaries are not understood by the people and in the great majority of cases these are artificial from the native's point of view. Tribal groups are split down the middle in many areas; one half may be in Iraq and the other half in Iran. The Middle Easterner has for centuries felt a strong loyalty to "his" group, but he felt free to change these loyalties unless subjugated by a larger force. The great empires, such as the Turkish, Byzantine, etc., maintained themselves by setting tribe against tribe. In these strong centrally controlled organizations there were no sharply drawn geographic boundaries. Villages allied themselves with Baghdad or Byzantium, depending on which could provide them with the best and safest life at the least cost. There is not now, and never has been, a great concern for the welfare of the larger power groups among the non-urbanized, non-Western-educated population. Instead there has been only concern for one's local group and the combined self-interest of the confederated groups. The Kurds, for example, would like to be reunited into a whole, but free to align themselves with Ankara, Baghdad or Tehran to further their own best interest as the circumstances of the time might dictate. But the artificial boundaries drawn by European powers bind a fraction of the Kurds to Turkey, another portion to Iraq and the remainder to Iran. Thus all three are doomed to be relatively ineffectual minorities in each country. The struggle for power in Turkey in the late 1950s was essentially a struggle between the cities, which were moving rapidly toward further urbanization, and the peasants in the villages which comprised about two-thirds of the total population, who remain firmly attached to their traditional culture.

The school systems in the urban centers preach loyalty to the nation—a concept that has little meaning for the older people and villagers who never see a school. In 1960 two out of every three school-age children in Turkey were not in school and the situation is much worse in many other places in the Middle East. Despite compulsory education laws, there simply are not enough seats in the schools, or teachers, and as a result this situation is likely to exist for many years. One serious problem is the population which is increasing at a far greater rate than the educational facilities.

The political parties have become pawns in the age-old pattern of confederation against confederation, family against family. The two bodies in the struggle in Turkey were the Democratic and Republican parties. Each attempted to obtain the peasants' support until the Democratic Party found itself in the position of being so dependent on them that it was forced to forego some of its progressive ideas, and actually began to undo some of Kemal Ataturk's reforms. When the peasants appeared to be getting the upper hand, returning Turkey to a traditional Moslem state, the cities turned to their one strong suit, the Turkish Army. These are natural results of a power structure on which these people have relied for centuries. It would have been much more complicated had not most of the people within the boundaries of modern Turkey at the time considered themselves to be Turks. The only significant minority in Turkey is the Kurds, about 12 per cent of the total population, but they played no serious part in the revolution of 1960.

The factors which underlie the Middle Eastern power structure are many and varied, and they will not disappear in a generation. Education for all the people over a period of many years with heavy exposure to outside cultures appears to be the best remedy.

The importance of the family group and the freedom of this group to change loyalties make the formation of permanent nation-states extremely difficult. Turkey is much more stable than most nations in the area because a single ethnic group dominates. Ataturk understood the traditional loyalty structure and created a nation that at least had a fighting chance to become a cohesive cultural unit. What was said earlier about the Kurds wishing to shift alignment between Ankara and Baghdad is equally true for dozens of other minority groups throughout the Middle East. As a further complication, smaller groups feel free to change their "ethnic" affiliation, as impossible as this may sound to a Westerner. Some Persians consider themselves presently to be a part of the Qashqai confederacy (basically a Turkish group)[19] and could change this if it were to their advantage. The age-old system of protecting oneself by joining opposing power groups has a built-in, natural instability, which is compounded because a large portion of the population is nomadic. The average Middle Easterner (which by definition does not include the considerable number of Western-educated men and women) feels no more loyalty to the central governments (except possibly in Egypt) than he has felt to the changing confederations to which his group has belonged throughout the centuries. Central authorities are barely able to maintain themselves in power by the use of well trained and equipped armies as they attempt to enforce submission to the central governments.

As a result concentration of effort in the power struggle has merely shifted its focus so that now competing groups work to gain control of the military. Hence the great number of military coups in recent years. The small number of Western-educated leaders do not seem to understand the traditional dynamics underlying this struggle. Most of them attempt to destroy the age-old power structure rather than work through it for a gradual and more effective change which might be permanent. Few of these men educated in the West seem to realize that destruction of opposing groups has no effect on the subconscious value systems which determine the actions of the great majority of the people. This reaction to any threat to the small local groups is a natural one, and it will take many years to teach the masses that a strong central government can give them the security they want without taking away their freedom of choice, and the governments must show that they are willing to do this. Actually most governments have acted in such a way as to indicate to the man in the street that the old power struggle is still operative in its traditional form and his only protection is to react to the central authority as he has for centuries. A government which can convince the people that it can protect them without taking away their freedoms, and sets about the job honestly, might be able to succeed where so many have failed.

Most of the Western-oriented Middle Easterners I have known feel that they have, through their contact with the West, learned a better way of life. The Western-educated leader in the Middle East often does not consciously understand his reactions to particular situations, but the use of the army to settle disputes only reaffirms in the minds of most of the citizenry that a strong central government is to be feared rather than supported. This leads to more instability. The Israeli-Arab dispute is one of the strongest unifying forces in the Middle East because of the tradition of ethnic solidarity combined with the custom of putting aside disputes within smaller groups until the issues between ethnic units are settled. The Israeli-Arab struggle then can be seen as a force for uniting the Arabs, but it is complicated by divisive forces. For example, if the threat were removed, the power groups within Syria would once more increase their struggle for control of that government, increasing the instability there.

The West would do well to learn that the Middle East respects ability, and the Middle Easterners often shift their loyalties to be on the winning side if they can do this with no loss of "honor." If we want to keep them on our side, we should continually demonstrate our superiority so that they will feel safest in our camp, and we should avoid anything that hurts their honor. Actually many Turks with

whon I discussed this point were convinced that we
were doing just this, and they interpreted our actions
as a demonstration of power. Hesitation and com-
promise are regarded as signs of fear.

Many Americans tell me that we should spend
more money building up the economy of these
countries and less trying to impress them militarily.
The exact opposite is probably true. Since the
masses are uneducated and do not understand even
the simplest facts about the economics of an in-
dustrialized nation, we are likely to win more
friends (or at least supporters) if we show our
strength and refrain from interfering with their
traditional small-group freedoms, even when these
appear to us to violate the rights of the individual.
Our concepts of individual freedom are not shared
by many Middle Easterners. Freedom to them is the
freedom for their group to do as it pleases. An
individual can rarely make a personal choice in his
own life, and the general consensus is that this would
be a bad thing if it were possible. Coupled with a
show of force and the permitting of local groups to
remain autonomous, we should spare no effort in
helping educate the masses to the inherent economic
and social advantages of stable nation-states. Perhaps this approach would bring some degree of
stability, a stability not based only on the military
power of a central government, but resting strongly
on the faith of the people. This will, however, take
many years to accomplish. The alternative, it would
seem, is a perpetuation of the traditional struggle
for power as it has gone on for centuries.

CHAPTER FIVE

The Supernatural

Another dominant factor in the life of any traditional Middle Easterner is his relationship with what a Westerner would label as the supernatural. Understanding the lack of a sharp distinction between the natural and the supernatural is important to an accurate evaluation of the people who live in the Middle East. This distinction is recognized by some city dwellers who have been educated in Western-style schools, but often even this is a very thin veneer. In trying to understand and deal with people in the Middle East, it is imperative that Westerners have some grasp of this traditional world-view, which contrasts so sharply with our own because here again we will find strong subconscious motivations which are radically different from the drives which direct the lives of people in most of Western Europe and the United States. The ability of a patriarch to call down curses on any recalcitrant member of his household is an example of the close interrelationship between the real world of everyday life and the supernatural.[1] There are many other such overlaps between the two worlds, some of which will be explored in this chapter.

There are many fairly comprehensive works on this subject. The reader interested in the world-view of traditional Islam should consult one of these.[2] However, since the area under discussion is predominantly Moslem and since religion almost everywhere is at least partially related to the "otherworld," we should say a few things about it. Fundamentally, Moslems wish to know the will of God (Allah) so that they can bend their lives in the right direction and thus move from this world into eternal paradise after death. Allah loves all who know and live by his "way," so that the good Moslem attempts to understand his will. Research in the physical laws of nature is not disapproved of, but it has no primary value for the people in the Middle East because life is so short.[3] Paradise, on the other hand, is eternal. Thus one should concentrate research on those things that concern the life hereafter. A great amount of scholarly energy has been applied to the study of the Koran and associated documents. The words of these scholars have for centuries been handed down by the religious teachers. The people, who do not consider themselves in a position to question those learned men, simply memorize what is passed on, and the devout ones attempt to live by these teachings.

This approach to learning and scholarship has resulted in Middle Easterners generally not taking readily to Western types of education. As an example, which could be multiplied a hundred-fold, during one year of teaching in the Middle East, 1 asked four essay questions on each exam. Three required only the return of information which I had given in lectures. The fourth necessitated the student's taking things he had learned and reassembling them to solve a practical problem he might be confronted with in the classroom when he began to teach. I do this with American students regularly and generally get acceptable answers. In this university-level institution, however, out of 100-plus students, I usually got only one reasonable answer and one or two very poor attempts. The other students refused to try, generally writing on their papers something to the effect that I had not given them the answer in class. This reaction indicated a basic philosophical approach to life, a part of the cultural heritage of the area since long before the birth of Mohammed.

This value was incorporated because it was basic to Mohammed's view of the world. The old ways were considered to be good, learned from people who were older than the student, who did exactly as the teacher instructed. There was no attempt to improvise or create new and better things. This lack of creative interest makes attempts at industrialization seem hopeless. I once asked a class to write an essay on "how to save time or energy," and the typical response was that they had no need to save time or energy; this might be important in America but not in the Middle East. They further amplified this by adding that if they saved time they had nothing in particular to do with it and that they would then spend more time walking in the garden. Despite this attitude, once young people are freed from this centuries-old dogma, they make excellent students and throw their energy behind movements for modernization of their countries. So far, however, this spirit has moved a relatively small minority and most of these "innovators" are very young. Many of these students become frustrated because the older men will not listen to their new ideas. After their university days they either leave the Middle East to seek work in the United States, Germany or Great Britain or may become members of various political factions which contribute to the unrest in the area, actually retarding the modernization they would like to promote.

The Middle East is a collection of what anthropologists call folk or traditional societies.[4] A striking characteristic of this type of culture is its religious nature. This does not mean that people living in traditional societies are more religious than other social groups, but that these people tend to equate their way of life with their religion. This is best understood when it is contrasted with urban societies which are regarded as more secular. In many cases the religion has little influence on the rest of the culture.[5] Since Western Europe and America are largely urban and the Middle East is largely folk, there is a wide area of misunderstanding between the contrasting societies.

One of the first points that must be stressed in any attempt by Westerners to understand Middle

Easterners is that each individual considers Islam as a way of life, not a religion which is a small part of a cultural whole. Further, one must also understand that there are quite different beliefs held by various groups, and each group believes that its way of life is Islam.

To understand these seeming contradictions one must delve a little further into the world-view of the vast majority of people in the area. Population figures in the Middle East are not very reliable, but roughly 70 per cent of the people are reported to live in small local groups. These are villages for the most part. From the peasant's perspective the world consists of two things: his valley and the outer world. The world he sees contains the agricultural property as well as the pastures used by the people of his village. He was born here, he will marry here and he expects to die here. Within the village there is usually a mosque and a religious teacher. Such teachers frequently spend nearly all of their lives in one village, and gradually Islam becomes equated with the local culture. The isolated, self-sufficient nature of these communities gives the peasant a feeling of security which is nearly impossible to duplicate anywhere else.

The tribes are also isolated, even though they are constantly on the move. Tribal isolation is a result not only of nomadism, but of a suspicion and distrust of outsiders. It is just as effective a barrier to understanding other peoples as the physical isolation of the villages. Even when contact occurs between a nomadic group and outsiders, there is the problem of communication. Few people outside the cities in the Middle East can read and write, and most cannot understand classical Arabic,[6] which is the language of the Koran. Turks, Iranians, Kurds and many other peoples in the area speak languages unrelated to Arabic. But even the majority of Arabs are not able to read the Koran and adjust their way of life to it. Many who memorize large portions of the Koran do not understand the Arabic they memorize and as a result knowledge of the Koran does not modify their way of life or act as an agent of cultural unification. They probably would not change their culture radically even if they did understand the Koran.

The world-view of the nomad would appear to be somewhat broader than that of the village, but it is broader only in the sense that the area he considers his personal world is slightly larger. He too dichotomizes the world into the area over which he migrates, often going out of his way to avoid an encounter with other groups, and the outside. His suspicion of outsiders is illustrated in the following quotes: "My major difficulty [in collecting ethnographic data] was the suspicious attitude of the people"[7]; "The peasants of Buarij consider their village a world of its own . . . as do all Lebanese villagers in varying degrees. . . ."[8]

Daniel Lerner has an interesting theory concerning culture changes in the Middle East which is pertinent at this point. Basically the theory states that the rate of change (from a traditional type of society to an urban culture) is directly proportional to the amount of contact with the outside world, either personal or through the radio, newspapers, movies, etc. This basic thesis seems to be valid for the Middle East despite some criticism of Lerner's methodology for studying the phenomenon and some of his conclusions. The observable changes over the past 20 years clearly show that those places with a high degree of interaction with the outside have changed at a much more rapid rate than those which have remained comparatively isolated (see Lerner's chapters on Balgat,[9] a Turkish village near Ankara, and my book *Life in a Turkish Village*).

The importance of Islam in the Middle East rests on the belief required of all people that Allah is the only God and that Mohammed was his prophet, the first pillar of Islam. Coupled with this is the belief that this life is temporary and that one must work toward an afterlife which is eternal. Islam is thought of as a way of life and all must strive to follow this "way" to assure a place for themselves in the paradise which follows death. One might think that this would result in a very homogeneous culture, but that is not the case. Everyone believes that the culture of his local group represents the nearest thing to a perfect Islamic way of life that is humanly possible. Every activity in a village is said to be done this way or that because of something that Mohammed said or did; and these may be made up on the spur of the moment. While one would expect this reasoning to shape all the cultures into an identical mold, it has not. There are, however, some basic similarities. Many customs

such as for weddings and funerals, are similar
throughout the area in certain basic respects such
as the payment of goods and possibly money to the
family of a bride, and the washing and handling of
a corpse for a funeral. The five pillars of Islam are
the same: (the first one was given in the introductory
sentence of this paragraph), (2) an annual fast of
one month, (3) giving alms to the poor, (4) prayer
to Allah five times a day and (5) a trip to Mecca,
the Hac (Turkish spelling), at least once during a
lifetime. These are considered necessary for a good
life, though needless to say everyone does not do all
of them regularly. Many other similarities, such as
the patrilineal extended families discussed earlier,
are attributed to Islam, but actually these things,
along with most of the material culture, were in the
Middle East long before Mohammed lived.

It might be well to consider what Westerners
would regard as the overlap of the natural and the
supernatural. The act of a father calling down divine
punishment on his dependents has been mentioned
earlier, but there are other ways to cause unnatural
things to happen. To list a few, women who wish to
become pregnant often utilize a wide variety of
charms; sick people call "healers" instead of the
local doctor. Frequently this is done by the so-
phisticated urbanites. Charms are always carried to
ward off the Evil Eye, and so on.

Probably the most widespread belief in the
Middle East concerns the Evil Eye, as it is to be
found almost everywhere. This is believed to cause
sickness and sometimes death. In Turkey it re-

portedly could be cast by evil people to make others sick. A famous physician once explained to me that the eye had the power to collect dangerous ultraviolet rays and then cast them forth at a later time on an unsuspecting victim. The belief is also common that a close friend or loved one can inadvertently cause the Evil Eye to afflict a person, particularly a child, by praise. The name of Allah is believed to be a protection against this evil, so that immediately after complimenting someone it is necessary to say, "Mashallah." *Mashallah* is usually translated by Turks as, "God bless you," but there is no equivalent in English for the term. An almost identical complex surrounds praise in Iraq.[10]

The name of Allah is believed to be a protection against evil of all kinds throughout the entire Moslem area, but other protections are widely used. Children, animals and even taxi cabs have blue beads attached to them as symbolic protection against the Evil Eye. In Morocco, when a woman is about to give birth to a child, the midwife fumigates the room to ward off the Evil Eye by throwing the intestines of a porcupine on an incense burner.[11] The child is swaddled very tightly and a cotton band with five vertical lines traced on it is wrapped around the child's head to protect it from the same curse.[12] In Turkey a small pin with a blue bead is affixed to the swaddling clothes as soon after birth as possible for the same purpose. In North Africa black appears to be the color most often used to ward off the menace, though henna, an orange-colored material, is also used. In the Asian part of the

Middle East the turquoise bead seems to be the strongest protection. The injunction, "Grace be to God," is repeated if someone says something nice to the mother of a child in Morocco, as it is elsewhere in the Middle East.[13] Compliments are supposed to bring evil because they make the inhabitants of the spirit-world jealous, and they get even by causing illness. Thus many villagers and nomadic tribesmen dress their children in rags and let them run about dirty so that they will not be afflicted by the Evil Eye if someone compliments a child without the customary "Mashallah." Is it any wonder that the Middle Easterners resist most efforts to institute good hygiene in the area! It is not just a matter of being dirty and not knowing better; being dirty is safer and more healthful than being clean. A beautiful child can attract the attention and jealous wrath of an evil jinn just by being beautiful.

Turks have told me that the people who are closest to a child and love it can, with a compliment, accidentally cause more harm than the casual visitor. They also say that certain people who have the power to cast the Evil Eye can actually kill on purpose, irrespective of the degree of relationship to the afflicted.

The Evil Eye, accidentally or intentionally cast, is suspected of being the cause of nearly all kinds of diseases. Treatment varies greatly throughout the area, but everywhere the name of God is thought to drive it away. My daughter has for years worn a pin with the word "Mashallah" in Arabic characters as the design. This is a beautiful piece of jewelry. These are worn by educated Middle Easterners today for decoration, but the peasants wear them as a protection against all of the ills which are associated with the Evil Eye. Often small replicas of the Koran or passages from it are worn for the same reason.

It is difficult for educated Westerners to understand the extent to which the illiterate peasant associates disease with magic or supernatural forces, or sometimes sees illness as a punishment for sin. My first experience with attempts to teach Middle Easterners the reasons for sanitation, particularly the placement of latrines away from and below the water supply, occurred in 1959 as a part of a renewed attempt by the Turkish government to eradicate illiteracy by a mass education project in the military. Three Turkish instructors from the Ministry of Education and I tried to explain what a germ was to a group of men who believed strongly in what they could see, but attributed nearly everything that they could not see to some kind of magic or evil spirit. The expressions on their faces clearly indicated that they thought that we had taken leave of our senses when we told them that diseases were caused by little creatures in the water which were too small for them to see. After all, "everybody knows. . . ." We found help from an unexpected source, however, because there seemed to be some difference of opinion as to just what everyone knew. This induced enough curiosity so that the students were willing to learn. Using a

19. Open-air market 35 miles from Karachi. There are
no women in the picture because they fled when the author
started to photograph them.

20, 21. Pakistani women in *purdah* (veiled). The costumes of these women are designed to prevent them from sexually stimulating a stranger, even by accident.

22. Pakistani men singing at a mosque where a Holy Man is buried. Such mosques are much sought after by the sick and by childless women.

23. Holy Man curing sick in a Pakistani mosque. Many Middle Easterners believe that illness comes as a punishment for sin or as the result of a curse.

24. Sultan Ahmet Cami in Istanbul. Built about 500 years ago, this structure is known as the Blue Mosque because of its beautiful blue and green tile decorations.

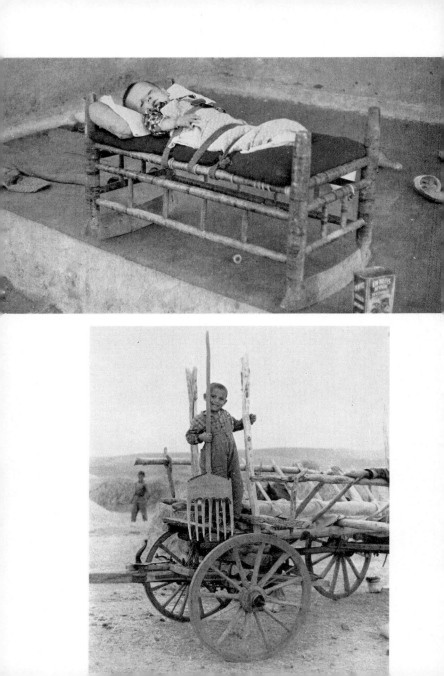

25. Turkish baby in a village cradle. Babies and young children are believed to be especially vulnerable to baleful supernatural forces.

26. Turkish village boy. One of the important events in the life of such a boy is his circumcision ceremony, which can take place any time between the ages of 5 and 12.

27. Author and his family with Demirciler family. To sustain the honor of a family or village, tradition requires lavish hospitality toward guests.

28. Village mosque in Demirciler, Turkey. Religious practices vary from village to village but each considers its way of life an ideal expression of Islamic belief.

microscope, we let them see what appeared to be clear water. Then they were convinced that there actually were millions of little things in the water they hadn't been aware of. They were still not convinced that germs caused disease, but they at least accepted germs as something else to worry about, along with witchcraft, punishment for sins and capricious spirits.

For an excellent description of a situation wherein a Western-educated Iranian attempted to help modernize the villages of her country, see *Reveille for a Persian Village*.[14] My own experiences with Turkish illiterate recruits were much similar to those described so well in this book for the Iranian village of Sarbadan. It is important to note not only how these people react to specific situations but the intensity of feeling regarding disease and the belief in various magical practices for cures. To deal effectively with the problem of disease in the Middle East, the cultural elements associated with these beliefs and feelings must be understood by technicians who can then use these beliefs to their advantage instead of antagonizing the peasant and making an enemy of him by ridiculing his beliefs. While no one really gives these cultural factors the consideration they deserve, it was my experience that Westerners were generally more sympathetic to such an approach than were educated Middle Easterners. After all, the villager knows from his own observation that most people who consult the local healers live. That the great majority of these sufferers would have lived without seeing the healer cannot be proved, but it is doubtless true. He notices that the majority of people who go to the healer get well, therefore the healer has cured them. He does not know whether the new "charms," shots, medicines, etc., of the Western-educated doctor will work or not, so he is naturally cautious. The Middle Easterner will accept new methods when it is shown that these are more effective than the old, but he is afraid of the unknown. The peasant must be shown that the new medicines work and do no harm. Then and only then will he accept them.

Another interesting part of the folklore of the Middle East is the "jinn," called genie in English, a spirit capable of assuming any size, shape or form, which lives in unusual places. Such places are generally frightening and are avoided by those who believe in these creatures. These spirits often cause trouble, but they can also bring pleasure. In Morocco they are described as "fond of desert places, of drains, of lavatories, ruins, and cemeteries. They come up to the surface of the ground at night . . . [and] one should be very careful not to offend them."[15] " . . . Every human being has his double . . . whose . . . life is exactly the same as his human counterpart."[16] In Lebanon they say that "the haunts of . . . jinn are primarily waste lands. . . ."[17] From Afghanistan Schurman reports that, "aside from formal religious beliefs, there are the almost universal beliefs in jinn . . . malevolent spirits hovering around certain areas."[18] These creatures are thought almost everywhere to be able to assume any size or shape, and they are commonly seen as domestic animals. Reports of jinn accosting men in the guise of beautiful women can be found in many places.[19] Such jinn are supposed to be of unsurpassed beauty and they attempt to seduce the men. If a man yields to this temptation he is killed when the sex act is completed.

In Iraq, as in Morocco, every person is thought to have a double which is a jinn.[20] The details are different, but considering the geographic area, ranging from Morocco to Afghanistan, one would not expect them to be exactly the same. These creatures are similar in all areas in that the fate of individuals is connected with that of the jinn. The creatures like to live in the same kinds of places, and they are frequently found in the shape of domestic animals. One must be very careful not to offend a jinn for fear of dire consequences such as bodily injury or disease. The jinn also appear to have a sense of humor as they "will play practical jokes on human beings in order to have fun at their expense. If a young girl pleases them, they do not hesitate to carry her off."[21] These creatures everywhere appear to dread the name of God and the injuction "Bismillah" (a word which is derived from Allah, God) is used to scare them off so that one does not inadvertently injure one and incur his wrath.

Several things about the jinn point up the close interrelationship between the natural and supernatural. These creatures are certainly different from the ordinary in that they can take animal, human and sometimes other forms at will, yet they appear to be born and die, like people and animals, and in Morocco they live the same life as their human counterparts. They get angry and knock people down, injure or even kill them, and also they play practical jokes on mortals for amusement. Thus they are both natural and supernatural at one time, indicating once more that the Western categorization of the world does not match or even parallel that of the Middle East. Fuller emphasizes that in Buarij, Lebanon, "the sacred and secular aspects of life are interwoven."[22] Understanding this, which is reported by almost all field workers, is an important part of understanding the culture of the area.

The Middle Easterner's fatalistic approach to life is emphasized by Westerners, and is illustrated by a quote: "When all the birds were gathered together to make their final arrangements before starting on a pilgrimage to Mecca, they passed a resolution saying: 'If God wills, we will start tomorrow.' But the hens cried out 'If God wills or not, we will start tomorrow.' When the time came to start they were punished for their irreverent words by finding themselves unable to fly."[23] This explanation as to why hens don't fly is illustrative of what can happen to one if he does not accompany any proposed activity with the required "Insallah" (Turkish spelling). Westerners usually interpret this type of story as proof of fatalism, but it really illustrates a punishment for opposing God's will. In reality Middle Easterners are afraid of opposing God's will, and a careful examination of their beliefs shows much that is not fatalistic.

"Insallah," the formula which the hens omitted, is usually thought to be equivalent to "if God wills." This is the translation given in many dictionaries and by those bilinguals with whom I have spoken on the subject. However, this translation implies a much stronger sense of predestination than I have found in the general pattern of life for most Middle Easterners. If all things were preordained, that is, life and death, sickness and health, etc., why would the people spend so much time and effort on charms? If it were preordained, then it could not be altered and efforts to stay healthy and alive would be futile, but the people quite obviously believe that they can change the course of events. Their attitude seems to be that people cannot go against the will of God without suffering some punishment, and if one attempts to do so, his effort is foredoomed to failure. Therefore, a Middle Easterner has two reasons for being cautious about new undertakings: (1) fear of punishment and (2) the certainty of failure if it conflicts with God's will because if God does not want something, then it will not be. However, by saying, "Insallah," he is saying, "if this does not conflict with the will of God, I'll do it." This translation seems to show the real feelings of the people in the Middle East, as reflected by their actions, much more clearly than, "if God wills," because "to will" indicates that God has a "plan." There seems to be little evidence in the lives of Middle Easterners that they believe in a "plan," but rather that God has a number of "don'ts," some of which are not clearly known. Hence one must protect himself from coming into direct conflict with God, because man will always be the loser.

If the above translation of "Insallah" is valid, why are Middle Easterners so reluctant to try new things? Why do they just sit and wait for things to happen? One is tempted to attribute this attitude to fatalism and say that Middle Easterners believe that everything is preordained. Therefore one needs only to let things happen in due course. This certainly does not seem to be in line with the observable facts. The basic philosophy seems to be that if one does something already tried and found good, he is relatively sure that God approves, but if something new is tried it may or may not be what God wants. If you try something that is new and it fits in with the Islamic way of life, all is well. If, however, you try and it does not, then you will fail and you may even be punished for your presumption. Therefore, given this basic premise, isn't it only reasonable to stick to the old things that have been proved rather than take a chance on being punished for trying something new? The little word, "Insallah," accompanies plans simply to indicate that one is not flouting God's will and to protect a person from punishment in case his plans conflict with those of God.

In a Middle Eastern city, around 1930, a man decided to build a flour mill because the wheat from the region around the city was shipped several hundred miles, ground into flour and then shipped back. A German engineering firm was hired to build the plant, which called for a number of "safety devices." The native engineers saw no need for these expensive devices because if someone got hurt it would be a sign of God's displeasure. Hence safety devices could not possibly be of value. The plant was completed without the safety equipment, and during the first month of operation the managing director's son fell into a flywheel and was killed. This was interpreted as a sign from God that He did not wish this mill to be there, so it was closed. It remained closed for over 30 years before the government bought it. Even the government did not reopen it where it was. The plant was dismantled and reassembled in another city. This story illustrates the effects of these beliefs on the economic life of the people.

Understanding the difference between a belief in predestination and the actual situation in the Middle East can make the difference between understanding what is happening there today and failing to understand. New ideas should be tried out under conditions that are as nearly identical with those in the Middle East as possible, and then the ideas with the proof should be presented to the peasants. Under such circumstances it is highly probable that the new techniques, institutions, etc., will be adopted and utilized almost immediately. The approach by the central governments is also wrong, because God's punishments are more certain and severe than those of the authorities. In most cases force will not work because the peasants will simply wait and see what is going to happen rather than pitch in to make a project a success. Lack of enthusiasm is likely to be as disastrous for a project as direct opposition. If a Middle Easterner knows that the idea has been tried and has worked, then it must be acceptable to God, and he will work hard for it.

This attitude is inculcated in children at an early age in the form of reprimands when the child fails to say "Insallah." The children also absorb these values from the folklore. Stories such as the one explaining why hens do not fly are common, and the theme of "not offending God" occurs with monotonous regularity.

The belief that a good deal depends on God's blessings, rather than on one's efforts, accounts also for what Westerners sometimes regard as the Middle Easterner's very unrealistic approach to goals. As a typical example, in discussing the literacy program in Turkey, the Prime Minister (Adnan Menderes) said in a political speech one day that our group would have the program in operation by May 1, 1959, "Insallah." This pronouncement immediately went throughout the nation in the newspapers and on the radio. The odd part of the whole thing was that the Prime Minister never asked the committee directing the program anything about possible starting dates. We first heard about it in the newspapers. At the next meeting of the committee, we were informed by the chairman that the program would begin on May 1. I pointed out that if

everything went perfectly, it would be the end of
June or early July before any textbooks would be
ready, and we had no buildings in which to hold
classes. Despite my comments, everyone tried
to get things ready for the May 1 starting date.
Later another man came from the United States.
He studied the project carefully and showed that
it would be physically impossible to begin the
program on May 1. His study did indicate that
November 1, 1959, would be a probable time.
This would permit us to have everything ready to
function smoothly. After much consultation, it was
decided that if one center could be opened in May,
preferably near Ankara, so that everyone would
see that the Prime Minister's schedule had been
met, this would be sufficient. One center did open
with two classes of 25 students each on that date
but with no equipment, and it was early July before
any supplies were available. The American target
date of November 1 proved to be a very accurate
one, as we had almost everything we needed to run
the schools properly by that time. Prior to that, the
classes were just assembling and passing time—not
actually functioning to teach the men to read and
write as the project had been designed to do.
Despite this shaky beginning, the program proved
to be one of the better ones run by the Economic Aid
Mission in Turkey.

The setting of unrealistic goals happens often in
the Middle East. This is due perhaps to a lack of
experience in planning for future contingencies, but
it may also be the result of a feeling that whatever

God wants will come easily and what he does not want will not happen regardless of one's efforts. I had the feeling that the Turkish members of the committee did not believe that our efforts alone would produce results, and that the reasons given by myself and the other American advisor for not starting the program until November were completely irrelevant. The one important point was that the "honor" of the government would suffer if the program did not start as announced. Their attitude seemed to indicate that we should get it started as quickly as possible and see if it worked, rather than make sure that it would work by proper planning before it began.

Lest one think that education erased these basic beliefs, I once talked to a doctor who had ministered to a pilot after a plane crash, performing a series of delicate operations. He explained after it was over that if God had not wanted the man to live he would have died. Here again, I think, we can see clearly that these people are not fatalistic, because if they had been, they would have left the pilot in the condition he was found and let God put him back together. On the other hand, if they believed in their own abilities, the doctor would have taken at least some of the credit for his wonderful feat. In dealing with the leaders of the Middle East, Westerners must realize that these deep-seated values are not erased by a veneer of Western education. They may or may not disappear after several generations of mass education, but they are still very effective controls on the direction and on the speed of cultural change in that area today.

The people of the Middle East, however, do attempt to influence the future. For instance, charms are believed to alter the course of events. One of the greatest tragedies for women is barrenness; those so affected are unceasing in their efforts to overcome the condition. In Iraq such women make a pilgrimage to the tomb of some unknown man and put up a small white flag.[24] They vow that if they become pregnant, they will do a good deed, such as care for a poor child, feed a beggar, etc. I have seen the ruins of old mosques in Turkey, the burying grounds for important men, with hundreds of little white strips of cloth fluttering in the breeze, the result of such pilgrimages. Such pilgrimages are also made to places as far away from Turkey as Morocco.[25] This does not show a fatalistic resignation to a preordained life.

Since most of these people are illiterate, one might wonder how they know these are tombs of famous men. I once asked a peasant in Ürgüp, Turkey, about this, and he looked at a smallish dome-shaped tomb and said that only a famous man would have a tomb such as that. It turned out that this burial was dated about 1300 A.D., and that no one in the village knew anything about it except that it was the tomb of a famous man, and that it was a good place to tie the little white flags when one wanted to become pregnant.

Possibly the most popular method of trying to alter the course of events in the Middle East is the use of a prayer or magic formula, sometimes written directly on the person (in Morocco for a specific disease)[26] but usually on something else, which is then carried or worn on a chain for protection. The "Mashallah" pin which my daughter wears is one example which could be duplicated in almost any Moslem country. In Iraq the favorite talisman is a small Koran in a gold case, and of lesser strength, though believed to be very effective, are the "names of God" or words from the Koran.[27] In Persia these written talismans are called *do'a* and are useful in protecting one against the Evil Eye as well as helping one achieve success in almost any venture.[28] The point is that it is believed that these cannot help you against the will of God, but it seems rather clear that the people feel that these can help where one is not directly in conflict with God.

One interesting type of charm is designed to change the emotions or actions of another person, as opposed to warding off evil spirits. One which I saw in operation is a charm to make someone love you. These are reportedly very common among the women. If a woman wants a man's love, she spreads fish oil around a door through which he must pass. Then he will lose the love he has for someone else and it will go to the person who put the fish oil there. We encountered this one day when our next door neighbor came out of her house screaming. After she calmed down, she explained that she had found fish oil on her door. When we did not understand what this meant, she explained that her husband had a mistress and that she was positive this girl had come around during the night and spread oil on the door so that her husband would leave her for the girl. This woman lived in a very modern section of Ankara, yet believed in the charm. Her husband had a fairly good job in the government so these beliefs are not found only among the illiterate peasants.

Descriptions of hundreds of such charms could be cited from the literature as well as personal experience, but the important thing here is that the number of charms, whether or not they are remnants of a pre-Islamic religion, strongly indicates that the peasants do not believe that everything is preordained. Hence they are not directly opposed to change, as is generally believed in the West, but rather they are suspicious and fearful of things that may or may not fit in with the will of God. This means, of course, that changes can take place without destroying the religion, if the people can be convinced that the new things are in line with the will of God, and this can best be done by showing that they really work.

One last example of the relationship between the natural and the supernatural comes from Mahmut Makal: "The hearth is the local solution for all illness. A pain in the knee, or cataract in the eye, a stomach ache—anything under the sun—off you go to the hearth. The most favoured hearth in our village is the Yılancık (sweet little snake) Centre. Not a day passes but somebody goes there. . . . In all these hearths every illness is attended to; but some have specialist branches, as famous doctors do. The blood-letting hearth is at a place called Kizilga-

ya (red stone). . . . The fever hearth is in the
village of Yuma. It is mostly there that they go.
People don't go to these hearths at random. It is
decided by divination. A little water is placed in a
pot. Needles are then placed in it, each pointing to
a village which has a hearth. The needle which
goes rusty first indicates which hearth will cure the
sickness."[29] Here, from a village in central Turkey,
we see still another indication of the overlap between
the natural and the supernatural. Disease is felt to
be caused by forces which cannot be understood.
Supernatural forces indicate—by rusting a needle—
which hearth can cure the disease, and at the hearth
anything from a prayer to an amulet can be prescribed as a cure. I do not know why Makal calls
these places "hearths." They are simply places
where sacred men able to cure people live.

So far it has been emphasized that there is no
sharp distinction in the Middle East between the
natural and the supernatural. We have seen the
Evil Eye as a cause of disease, jinn which do not
belong to this world but which interfere in it
constantly and the supernatural diagnosis and cure
of illnesses of many kinds. In general the traditional
Middle Easterner appears to think of the world as a
very large and unfathomable place, and I suspect
that it seems to him that our division into the
natural and the supernatural is quite arbitrary and
senseless. What we consider to be the "other world"
is to him just an extension of this one, and such
things as jinn, which live in this one, have all sorts
of unnatural abilities. These characteristics do not

appear to be restricted to any group or geographic area, though the manifestations do differ somewhat from region to region, as illustrated by the incidents reported from Iran to Morocco for villages, tribesmen and urbanites.

Makal's *Bizim Köy*.[2] The author states that while
the woman was convulsed with pain, the women
pushed and pulled her in every direction in an
attempt to bring the child out. He felt that it was a
"matter of chance," whether they were successful
or not, and "in most cases the child is either born
dead and the woman is saved, or they both make
the journey to the cemetery together." The editor,
in a footnote, states that the number of live births
is well over half, and this is certainly true, as shown
by Makal's own statistics of 36 per cent and 41
per cent of the village children dying before their
first birthday.[3] These figures are for two nearby
villages. This type of overstatement is typical.
However, one problem may be that of translation,
because the Turks almost never use the equivalent
for the English "most," which is *çoğu,* but use instead
the word *çok,* which means "many." Makal's description states further that the tortures suffered by
the mothers are indescribable and cites the large
number of "dark-eyed brides" who die in childbirth.
He quotes the old women as saying, "What can we
do to alter these things? The God, who watches
over her and loves her more than we do, gave her
life, and it is he who takes her back. . . ."

Until about 1950 infant mortality approached a
rate of 40 per cent, not all at birth but certainly
during the first year of life. Being born in the Middle
East does not ensure a normal life of reasonable
length as it does in the West. Of the village women
whom I knew personally in Turkey, most had had
from 8 to 12 children of whom only 4 to 7 lived

past early childhood. Sources indicate that the situation in Persia was almost identical in the late 1940s.[4] Both the figures on mortality, which are uniformly very high throughout the Middle East, and the description of a birth show clearly the contrast in the West and the Middle East.

The following description of a birth in Persia is fairly typical for villages in that country, except again for the severity of the labor. "There on a bed of clean rags lay a girl of 15 or 16. Her face was so contorted by pain that she scarcely looked human. Her knees were up . . . [with] a *chodor* over them like a tent. . . . 'The child gave a hand,' she [the midwife] said, 'I touched it with snow and it withdrew it . . . but now he wants to give a shoulder I think. He will surely break his neck but first he will kill the mother. . . !'" The author of the account gave the girl a shot, and the group rested for some time. Then, "The girl's eyelids lifted. She bore down. Madar-i-khadkhoda [the midwife] lifted the *chodor*. The top of a black-haired little head presented [itself]. In a few minutes there was the lusty cry of a newborn boy."[5] This description is unusual on at least two counts: (1) the birth was undoubtedly more severe than normal or the midwife would not have sent for help by the author of the description and (2) the medication would not have been available for the average non-city dweller. However, the salient features of the birth situation are: (1) the young bride on a bed of "rags" (these are usually fairly attractive things that we would call comforters); (2) no attendant present as a rule, except for one or two old women; (3) the result, in this situation, a high mortality rate for both mothers and children. The only help that the mother gets during the birth process appears to be in the form of pressure on her body by the midwife with a few mechanical aids such as touching a part of the protruding infant with snow, when the wrong portion of the body appears to be coming out first, in order to make it withdraw into the womb and try again to come out properly. Full accounts of births are not often found, but the Turkish one by Makal seems similar in its general outline to those in Persia, except that there was no medical help available in Turkey at the time Makal was there, and the villagers attempted to take the mother to a doctor in another town.[6]

No mention is made of treatment of the placenta in Turkey or Persia. This is mentioned because anthropologists are usually looking for some sort of treatment of this residual from the birth, as such ceremonials are quite common. In cities in Iraq births are also generally accompanied only by a midwife, and the placenta is sometimes thrown into the river. Iraqi Arabs are also said to bury the placenta occasionally to appease the jinn of the earth.[7] Another fairly complete description of birth comes from Morocco. "The confinement must begin secretively . . . and the midwife has to be fetched . . . she is careful to take harmel, a salt, and alum . . . and scatter them in front of her to propitiate the djinn. . . . She thus makes an offering to the good genie and disperses evil ones.

. . . When the woman feels her first pain a bed is made ready. . . . This sheepskin is spread directly on the ground. If the floor is tiled or cement, the midwife has to fetch a basketful of earth . . . for the blood . . . must be absorbed by the earth. After the child is born, the midwife gathers up the earth very carefully and buries it in the garden. . . . The midwife, after having prepared the bed, scatters salt in the four corners of the room, in the courtyard and in the water closets. . . . She fumigates the room with the dried intestines of a porcupine . . . to ward away the Evil Eye. . . . At her [the pregnant woman's] side she places a nail, a knife . . . a consecrated chaplet . . . a pair of scissors, an olive twig from Mecca . . ." and a large number of other small items all with magical significance. Then the woman is prepared by removing her bracelets, etc. Incantations are said by any who are present and a variety of charms are utilized to make the birth easier. The husband may be summoned to assist the mother if the baby won't come (presumably with pressure on her abdomen) and the girl may even be carried to the mosque in severe cases.[8] "The after-birth is buried then under the threshold of the house."[9]

The actual birth is not considered by anthropologists to be as significant as what happens to the baby, mother, afterbirth, etc., immediately after the child is born. Again in Morocco, the infant is told "Allah ou Kbar"[10] and given a short speech. Then a mixture of flour and henna is put on its navel, oil is rubbed on its body, and it is covered with henna. An old piece of wool with a hole in it becomes the child's first shirt which he wears until the day of name giving. The baby is bound up tightly with its legs stretched out and arms folded in front. Then a band of cloth with five vertical lines traced in *kohl* is bound tightly about the baby's head as a protection against the Evil Eye during the coming seven-day period when it is supposed to be very vulnerable. It is described as looking "like a mummy." These exact words were used by a Bedouin Arab in describing the swaddling practices of his people, though in Syria the arms are bound to the side rather than folded in front of the body. As soon as the women of the household know that the baby is a boy, three "ululations," high-pitched trilling sounds, are made. If it is a girl no such signal is given. Again, the custom is almost identical for Syrian Bedouin. In Syria the men are usually gathered in a tent some distance from the place of birth, and if a girl is born a silence is said to settle over the group, almost as if they were participating in a wake rather than a birth. This attitude is so strong that if a person comes into a tent and everyone is sitting silently, it is not uncommon to say something to the effect, "what's wrong, has a girl been born?"

One significant difference between Syria and Morocco in the practices surrounding birth is that in the latter the giving of a name is postponed for seven days whereas in the former a child must be named as the cord is cut by the midwife.

In both cases various charms are utilized as a

protection against the Evil Eye, and other un-
pleasant spirits. On the seventh day, in Morocco, a
lamb is sacrificed if the baby is a boy, and the child
receives a name. The Bedouin fear that a child
without a name will not be able to enter Paradise
should he die, because the Angel of Death won't be
able to find its records. With no knowledge of the
good and bad things that the child has done, how
could it possibly be admitted to heaven? Signifi-
cantly, both groups feel that their way is that of
Islam. It would seem that in Morocco there is a
very high death rate during the first seven days of
life, and the villagers would prefer not to give a
child a name until they are sure that it has passed
this critical period.

The data presented indicate that pretty generally
throughout the Middle East a child is swaddled very
tightly. This is a practical way of protecting small
babies from serious injuries, especially for nomads.
A child is constantly in danger from the camels,
goats, etc., in a nomadic group, but even in a
village, where one might think a child would be
comparatively safe within the walls of the home, it
is endangered by the fire which is in an open hearth
on the floor or at floor-level in one wall. This is
especially true when the mother wants to put the
baby near the fire in cold weather. When swaddled
there is no danger that the infant will roll into the
flames. This makes the baby into one tight, solid
piece with no worry about its neck, arms or legs, so
that one can pick it up, put it on a camel or hang it
in a tree for safety while the mother works.

Parents make special efforts to protect small children from the Evil Eye and bad jinn. East of the Mediterranean this usually is done with blue beads, small copies of the Koran encased in gold or silver or charms which are worn about the child's neck. A basic difference in the practice between this portion of the Middle East and North Africa is the absence of a mention of blue beads in the descriptions of the latter cultures, and the use of *kohl* and charcoal in their place. Children in the Middle East are usually not punished physically. Babies remain swaddled until well past what Westerners would consider the age at which they should learn to walk. This is for their protection and also the convenience of the mothers who have heavy work loads. There may be other reasons, religious in nature, to justify the practice.

The fortieth day after birth is an important one in Morocco,[11] Iraq[12] and Turkey.[13] The ceremonies differ somewhat from place to place, but the description from Morocco will illustrate generally what happens. Incidentally, the 40 days may be somewhat flexible, as a Bedouin informant said that the period of restraint from sexual contact with the husband was "until after the woman had completed one menstrual cycle." This could vary, but for a nomadic people who do not live by the calendar, it is close enough to 40 days to suffice. The Moroccan child is presented on the fortieth day to the holy saints who protect the community and especially to his particular guardian spirit. The mother goes to the public bath, and then both she and the child are dressed up and beautified with *kohl* and henna. Then a feast is laid out for friends who must partake of it to ensure that the child will be loved by everyone. Afterwards the child is taken to the shrines of the town in a joyful procession. The home is meanwhile fumigated, and the child is taken to the shrine of his patron saint along with tools that represent what the child will be when he grows up, e.g., tablets, if the parents want him to be a learned man, a hammer if they want him to be a carpenter, etc. These tools are left at the shrine as an offering. The holy man at the shrine cuts the child's hair, which is regarded as the important part of the ceremony.[14] After these activities the child is thought to be past the most critical danger from evil spirits, and the family resumes its normal life. However, the child will continue to be protected in various ways, but to a lesser degree. Saying "Mashallah" after any compliment is still necessary until maturity is reached. This 40-day period is quite likely the period in which large numbers of infants died in the past, and the protections are thus justified on the basis of observed experience.

In Lebanon, as Fuller points out, "Sweets are handed out to visitors at the birth of a male child. This may or may not be done at the birth of a daughter. Throughout life, the male offspring possesses more prerogatives than the female. . . ."[15] Fuller goes on to say that infants are especially vulnerable to jinn or evil spirits. The placenta is buried in front of the doorstep and the first soiled diapers are put in the air vent above the door. A blue bead is affixed to the child's hat to protect it from the Evil Eye, or something with holy writing is suspended about its neck for the same purpose. The infant is tightly swaddled for ease in handling. If a child is breast fed by a wet nurse, the children of the wet nurse are considered to be brothers and sisters of the child so that marriage to them would be incestuous. We can see, by comparing the descriptions from Iran, Turkey and Lebanon, that some birth customs are typical of all three countries, as they are of the general Middle Eastern area. The handling of the diapers in Lebanon reflects Western influence perhaps, because in other areas the pants are filled with sand and there are no soiled diapers as the sand is simply changed, leaving the pants themselves clean, so that the practice of putting the soiled diaper in the air vent above the door is unusual.

Circumcision is an important event in the lives of male children. The amount of data on this subject is probably directly proportional to its importance throughout the area. Many if not all groups consider a lack of circumcision as being tantamount to infidelity. In a Turkish village circumcision takes place between the ages of five and twelve, usually around eight. Usually several families have the ceremonies performed at the same time and share the cost, which includes feeding the entire village if the community is small, and large numbers of friends and relatives in larger places. In the morning of the day of the ceremony there is singing and dancing by the men while the women prepare the house and food. About midafternoon the boy is placed on a horse which is decorated with brightly colored cloth, blue beads, etc. The animal is led up and down the streets in the village and then back to the child's home. Here the *sünnetci,* a specialist, performs the operation after which the guests praise the boy and present small gifts.[16] In the cities the home of a boy to be circumcised takes on an air of celebration, and large numbers of friends and playmates are driven over the city in taxis before the operation. Frequently a party will be held for the boy in a night club, hotel or restaurant. A friend of mine, an army officer, had an army band playing outside his window while the operation took place.

In Morocco the ceremony takes place at about seven or eight years of age and includes a lot more interaction between the mother and child than in and around Turkey,[17] where it is predominantly a masculine affair. One wonders if this is not a result of cultural diffusion from Spain. Bedouin tribes do not usually have in their camp groups a man who can perform the operation, and when such a "doctor" is anywhere in the area he will be brought to the camp to circumcise boys between the ages of six and ten.

In Iraqi cities the operation takes place at about seven years of age. Typically, a child "in elegant clothes" was "paraded through the streets . . . riding a richly caparisoned horse. . . . A local band walked at the head of the procession. . . . The barber who was to perform the operation was waiting in a lower room. . . . The band . . . continued to play even louder than before . . . the operation was soon over. . . . The little boys lay down on specially prepared beds . . . and [were] made a great fuss over. . . . That night . . . the women of the family connection gave a huge party for all their friends."[18] There appears to be very little difference in the basic elements of the ceremony in Turkey and Iraq despite the one country being predominantly Arab and the other Turkish.

So far we have discussed a ceremony in a Turkish village and city, a Moroccan village and a nomadic tribe in Syria as well as a city in Iraq. Morocco is the most divergent, as we might expect, for it is on the periphery of the area. The customs—the age at which the operation is performed, special kinds of dress for the occasion, the trip around the community, performance of the operation in the afternoon, a time for congratulations from the community following the operation, with a party the following evening—appear to be nearly universal in the Middle East.

There is little information on what happens to girls as they grow up. This may, however, be a result of the fact that most fieldworkers have been men. With the marked segregation of the sexes, it is very difficult for males to get this kind of information; even the men in these cultures do not know what their women do most of the time. There is probably no ceremony connected with the onset of puberty, however, because the only mention of any kind which has come to my attention is the following concerning Lebanon: "A girl on first menstruating may embrace the large bellied jar in which flour is stored, so signifying her entry into womanhood. . . . "[19] Even this report does not indicate that this is very important, because it states that the girl "may," and Fuller adds that "this is an informal act witnessed only by the mother."[20] The life of young females is generally centered around minor household tasks, which gradually increase in complexity until the girls reach the age of marriage. Thus they learn by taking over more of the mother's chores without any point at which a ceremony marks their maturity. Several reports indicate that maturity comes at about age 15 but may be sooner or later. There is no indication that this is connected with the first menses. Similarly, boys also gradually learn the required skills from their fathers and paternal uncles, with the one major interruption in this development being the circumcision. This important ceremony for the boys is perhaps one more way of maintaining the supremacy of males.

Marriage is undoubtedly the most important ceremony in the life of any Middle Easterner (see Najafi, *Reveille for a Persian Village*, p. 83). Generally throughout the area a preference for marriage to a patrilineal parallel cousin (father's brother's child) is reported by many scholars. A brief look at the facts will show how prevalent this marriage form is. From Lebanon, Fuller says that "first-cousin marriage on the paternal side is the preferred Muslim marriage."[21] In Iraq a girl is said, "to be married to her first cousin,"[22] and though it was not explicit, I would guess that it was a father's brother's son.

These are both Arabic peoples and the Arabs generally appear to follow this marriage pattern. In the Egyptian village of Silwa in the province of Aswan a family dispute arose when a marriage was arranged between a boy and his mother's brother's child, because, "according to custom [the paternal uncle] had precedence over the maternal uncle."[23] However, when we look at non-Arabic peoples, such as the Kurds, we find that "any type of cousin [marriage] was denied. . . ."[24]

In Turkey any first-cousin marriage is prohibited in at least one village, rejected as being incestuous. The impression is that group-endogamy (usually village or local camp group) is the rule, yet there are many villages in Turkey which do not practice strict endogamy. One wonders how many of the thousands of communities which have not been systematically studied are endogamous. Even where father's brother's children are preferred as marriage partners, individuals frequently do not marry such relatives. In the Persian village of Davarabad, cousin marriage is "eminently preferable to more distant kin, but no marriage is thought so idyllic as that between children of brothers."[25] Marriages of this type are said to be "drawn in heaven."[26] One faction of the villagers favored marrying "someone other than relatives . . . because you collect a whole additional group of kinsmen. . . ."[27]

In general, most accounts from the Middle East seem to emphasize that the father's brother's children have first claim on females. Among some Bedouin groups such as the Rwalla and the Marsh

Arabs, refusal to acknowledge this claim usually leads to slaying.[28] However, the female involved can be released by her father's brother's son to marry someone else, indicating that many marriages with people other than father's brother's children probably occur. Of the Moghôls of Afghanistan, it is said that, "preferred parallel cousin marriage cannot be said to be the rule. . . . "[29] However, arrangements involving father's brother's daughters "seem to be the norm among wealthy Afghans of the cities."[30] These quotes show that in two communities, in fairly close proximity, one is fairly strict about patrilinear parallel cousin marriages, while the other permits, but does not insist on, this type of arrangement. The same situation exists in Turkey and Persia. Probably it applies to the entire area. It can be stated with certainty, however, that marriages generally favor close kindred, usually cousins and often the father's brother's children.

Important preparations for a Turkish wedding in Demirciler were the agreement on (1) the fact that both families think that the marriage would be a good thing and (2) the financial arrangements necessary to make it legal, i.e., the amount of money and goods that the father of the bridegroom will give to the father of the bride. It is taken for granted that the bride's parents will provide an amount roughly equivalent for the wedding feast and household goods for the new couple. The custom in the Persian village of Davarabad is almost the same, except that an amount must be specified to be paid if the girl is divorced.[31] This payment does not enter into the negotiations in Demirciler because, it was stated categorically by all informants, divorce was not permitted in the village, and I found no evidence that there had ever been a divorce. A man who divorced his wife would be disinherited and expelled from the community. The Moghôls of Afghanistan are reported to have a ceremony which "is divided into three stages: (1) the marriage agreement . . . marked by an exchange of gifts by the two fathers. All negotiations take place in the home of the bride. (2) The exchange of the bride price, and (3) the actual marriage itself."[32] In Morocco marriage is said to be a "contract between families. . . . The arrangements . . . are made on the initiative of the boy's father. Ideally, the father locates a prospect and the rest of the family judge her. . . . A significant part of the arrangements is the transfer of cash, foodstuff, and a pair of slippers from the groom's family to the bride's."[33] In Lebanon, "parents theoretically arrange a marriage, a *wali* or 'go-between' acting in all formal arrangements."[34] In describing a particular marriage in Silwa, Egypt, Ammar says, "The father of the boy and his relatives and friends went to the house of the girl's father asking for her hand for their son. . . . Neither the boy nor the girl was present during this gathering for writing the contract."[35] Arrangements for marriages throughout the Middle East appear to be very similar in that the children have no say, at least theoretically; marriages are in reality contracts between two families. Usually initial contact is made by a go-between, the father of the boy initiates the procedure and a bride price must be paid. Generally an amount roughly equivalent to the bride price must come from the family of the bride to help set up the new family. In all cases the "actual marriage" takes place several months (often about a year) after the initial agreement. The initial agreement, however, is considered legally binding on both parties and failure of either side to complete the marriage is a disgraceful thing. I have witnessed a few of these broken "engagements" and the insult is felt keenly by the aggrieved side. Among the Kabyles of Algeria a father may negotiate and reach an agreement for his children, regardless of their age. I have heard Middle Easterners discuss the possibility of marriage for a small boy before his intended mate was born. Approaches were made to my wife for the hand of my daughter in 1956 when she was about eight years old. The weddings are not consummated until after the girls are 13 or 14, but contracts could have been negotiated and signed at any time.

The above described sequence is widespread in the Middle East, so let us examine briefly a hypothetical marriage following this pattern. The father of a young man or woman indicates that it is time to find a spouse for his child. Perhaps it is felt in their village that marriage should occur before the young man leaves for his military service. This is often done to prevent the young men from contracting a marriage away from home with some city girl through a civil ceremony which would disrupt the social organization in the local group. The family will

discuss the girls and boys they know who are properly related and have the proper social status, etc. In
many groups, but not in all, the husband-to-be's
family begins the negotiations. When it is decided
that a particular person is the best available, a go-
between is sought to make inquiries of the other
family, because of fear of loss of honor by a direct
refusal. This go-between is often an aunt. If the
young girl's father is amenable to the marriage, the
parents of the boy will make several visits to the
home of the girl. She is expected to treat these
visitors with great respect and display her ability to
be a good wife, mother and daughter-in-law. I have
known cases where the girl sabotaged what she
considered an undesirable marriage by doing dis-
respectful things during these visits so that the
callers would not want her as a wife for their son.
This disrespect can be subtle, such as crossing her
legs when her father and mother aren't looking or
smoking a cigarette. Being turned down at this
stage of the negotiations is likely to reflect on the
girl's reputation and make it difficult for her to be
married off later, and she risks the punishment of
her parents, should they find out what she has done.
However, a girl would not risk this unless the
marriage in question were intolerable to her. Thus it
can be seen that the girls are not completely helpless
in this situation.

When both families have agreed to talk the matter
over, which means in effect that all concerned are
satisfied with the arrangement, the groom's father
and mother will go to the home of the bride, where

most of the bargaining will take place. When both
sides are in agreement as to the financial and other
responsibilities of each party, a sum of money and
goods is given to the family of the bride. Reciprocal
gifts are required from the family of the bride, but
usually at a later date. After the bride price (the
goods and money given to the parents of the bride)
has been paid, a party is held which binds both
families to the marriage. This bride price is required
by Moslem law to make a marriage legal, though
the practice is not observed in some places today.
Some students say that such an exchange of gifts
makes the marriage more stable because the break-
up of a marriage would require the return of a
considerable amount of goods or money. This probably deters some husbands from seeking a divorce,
especially those in the poor areas. After the signing
of the contract, months, even years, may pass before the wedding takes place. The final ceremony,
a period of feasting and merry-making, terminates
with the test for virginity, after which the new
couple live together as man and wife.

The life of a man is not radically altered after his
wedding, as he will still live near his father's home,
if not in the same house, and will have few new
responsibilities after the wedding. Since most important matters are decided by his family, there is
little change in his daily routine. For the girl, however, there is a radically new regime. She leaves
her home where she had few responsibilities and
goes into an alien home where she will frequently
be treated almost as a slave by the older members

of her husband's household. Here she must do everything perfectly to uphold the honor of her family and prove that she is a good wife. When the marriage is the preferred patrilineal parallel cousin (father's brother's child) type, the strain is less on the girl than when it is not, since she enters a familiar family which already has an emotional attachment toward her. However, a large number of marriages must be with non-relatives, and in such cases the girl's adjustment is far more difficult. Fuller says that "the least popular of marriages is when a girl is married into another village."[36]

The real change in status comes when the couple has a child, especially if it happens to be a boy. The young bride is then relieved of many of her duties in serving the other members of her husband's family.

The major events in the ceremonial life of the young couple consist of regular religious holidays and the birth, death and circumcision of their children. Occasionally divorces and new marriages take place. Divorce is usually simple throughout the Middle East for men and almost impossible for women. The little phrase, "I divorce thee," must be repeated before witnesses three times by the husband. Traditionally, a woman's only recourse if she desired to break up a marriage was to antagonize the husband until he divorced her. According to Moslem law the marriage contract should contain a stipulation as to the amount due the woman if she is divorced. In many places the marriage is not considered valid if such a clause is not included in the contract as a protection for the woman. Payment is made in money, animals or goods by the man's family to the girl's father and she returns to her family home. In Davarabad, Iran, the woman forfeits this payment if she initiates the divorce action.[37] In Morocco, "a husband can divorce his wife for any reason whatsoever and the wife has no opportunity to contest it."[38] In Egypt, "the right and power to divorce one's wife is a part of the male ethos...."[39] Dorothy Van Ess says that in Iraq, "the husband says 'Thou art divorced,' three times. After the first and second sentences he can change his mind, but it is irrevocable after the third. . . . A husband may divorce his wife without any misbehavior on her part. . . . A divorced woman usually returns to her father's house."[40] These quotes describe the general pattern of divorce for much of the area.

Though the above method of dissolving marriages is reported from widespread places as typical, it is difficult to obtain actual descriptions of divorces which occurred when fieldworkers were in the area, even in otherwise fairly detailed accounts such as the one by Robert C. Alberts in "Social Structure and Culture Change in an Iranian Village" or any information as to rate of divorces. In Demirciler, Turkey, those questioned insisted that divorce was not tolerated under any circumstances. The lack of descriptions may result from the fact that divorce is not really as common as it is thought to be, or it may be simply the chance factors which regulate what a fieldworker witnesses. Breaking up a marriage is an intensely personal thing involving all sorts of stresses, personal and cultural. During the six and one half years which I spent in Turkey, I heard indirectly of several divorces, all but one among highly Westernized families. The one traditional Turk who was divorced had had a wife and one day we noticed that she wasn't around anymore. His explanation was that he had, "sent her back to the village," which meant, of course, that she had been divorced. I could get no details concerning the break-up, but I have the impression that no one really knows much about the frequency of divorce, only that it is easy. The assumption that it is easy must explain the belief that it is frequent. Fuller says specifically that "divorce is uncommon in the village"[41] (Buarij). It would be interesting to have sufficient data to know just how frequently divorce actually occurs among the traditional families. Many Middle Eastern friends of mine have told me that in their families it just doesn't happen, and my own experience would indicate that it is easy in theory, but infrequent, because families do not like to have their reputations tarnished by divorce.

Divorce is generally more common among the Westernized urbanites than among folk populations, and many of the statistics come from the cities, as the nomadic camp groups and villages are relatively inaccessible. By statistics, I mean only reliable figures on the approximate number of marriages in a given social group which actually end in divorce. Numbers would be valuable regarding other aspects of the culture too. For example, in understanding the difference between "ideal" and "statistical" norms for a cultural group, figures would indicate just how strong certain motivations are. If in 20 years only one girl is killed by her father or brothers for having lost her virginity, and several cases are generally known to have occurred, then the statistical norm is far from the ideal. The ratio of actual murders by close relatives in cases of adultery would indicate the strength of this particular norm in controlling the behavior of the average person. Fuller describes one situation in a Lebanese village wherein a woman was caught in the act of adultery with a young man. The act is punishable by death in the village by stoning, but nothing was done about it except that the young man beat her. Later she bragged about the incident to other women and said that the beating was nothing. [42]

Statistics on life expectancy as with other matters are unreliable throughout the Middle East. As an example, my family was counted four different times in the census taken in Turkey in 1955. This was not an unusual case, but typical, as the government liked to show high figures for almost everything except crime. Once I asked a member of the Turkish General Staff about a certain kind of technician whom we needed for the Literacy Project, and the officer said that he would ask his field commanders to find out if there were any. Each commander then asked his subordinates if they had such a technician in their units. The point is that there is no "bureau" where statistical information is kept, even for the military, nor is it considered to be of great importance. Further, I believe that most governments in the area manipulate figures to prove their points, and most politicians do not want reliable statistics for fear that these might refute their claims of improvement. Once while looking through government reports on roadbuilding in Saudi Arabia, I noticed that the government had appropriated large sums of money for roads each year, yet no appreciable number of new roads could be found. This sort of thing is common in the Middle East, in almost all aspects of political life.

Despite the lack of statistics, the life expectancy seems to be not much higher than 45 years. The actual statistical figure is undoubtedly much lower because of the high percentage of deaths during the first year. In Turkey if a person lives past the first two or three years, his chances of reaching 40 are pretty good. But there is a high death rate in the late forties and fifties, so that very few people live to be really old.

Death probably requires the greatest adjustment on the part of the dead person's relatives. In small folk societies the social responsibilities, especially of older men, are felt to be essential to a proper functioning of the culture and hence must be taken over almost immediately by someone else. Redistribution of possessions and prerogatives of the dead person frequently leads to quarrels among survivors, and it is important to the society to have conventions which reduce this friction so that it does not disrupt the social order.

Islamic law requires that the body be buried before sunset on the day following the death, but there are many things that must be done before the burial. In Sarbadan, Iran, a procession goes to the house for washing the corpse on the morning after the death. The men carry fuel for heating the water and the sons and nephews bear the body on a carpet. The mother comes last, the only woman in the procession. If the mother is dead there must be a substitute. The woman carries a package of white cotton cloth, and the body is carried through the "door of life" and placed on a stone table, where it is washed by the men of the village. The big toes are bound together, a bandage is placed over the eyes, and the mouth is filled with cotton. Finally, the body is anointed with perfumes and then wrapped in a large square of white cotton cloth. Everyone is required to help so that all will remember that any day can be the end of life. The body is then carried out the "door of the dead" to the burying place. The men all chant "La Elahalla Allah" (which means "there is no God but Allah") and every man hearing the chant is expected to bring his shovel and join the procession. The grave is quickly dug and the body placed therein. A stone is placed at the head and feet, and stones on each side of the head with one over the face to protect it. Then the earth is replaced. For three days the family holds open house in honor of the dead. The first day is for relatives, and the second and third for friends who pay their respects to the family.[43] This description applies in general, but there are regional variations. Most villages have a house for washing the dead, but many places do not have this convenience. Najafi describes a touching scene which she witnessed as a child in Abadan, Iran. "Kneeling beside the pool was a woman . . . washing a child . . . perhaps nine or ten . . . the mother . . . was preparing him for burial according to the Moslem religion. . . . When she washed a cheek she laid her own cheek against it and her crying rose a little higher. I saw her straighten the dark locks of his hair with her fingers, and finally wrap him in a piece of old muslin. Later, an older boy stepped from the shadows and helped the woman . . . carry the child away. . . ."[44] Najafi also reports that when she arrived in Sarbadan in 1955 the families were washing the bodies in the irrigation canals.[45]

In Morocco, "A corpse is washed with soap and water and dressed in new white cotton clothing and covered with a shroud of the same material. On the day following the death, the burial takes place. . . . The body is . . . put on a litter and carried to the cemetery, followed by the procession of mourners. The body is placed in a shallow grave and the grave is filled."[46] These descriptions emphasize the importance of (a) quick disposal of the body, partly a result of the climate wherein an unembalmed corpse will soon decay, (b) the ritualistic washing, which may or may not actually be cleansing and is sometimes accompanied by anointment with oils and perfumes, and (c) the required assistance of all males in the society. These three elements generally characterize the Middle East. Many people, especially the affluent, wish to be buried in the extensive graveyards surrounding famous shrines, and make contracts with a special group of caravaneers who haul bodies to burial grounds, sometimes many miles away. From the description of these unusual caravans, one is advised to stay some distance away because of the odor, as it may take several days to reach the burial place.

In the rites described the corpse is usually disposed of quickly and simply when compared with American funerals. The solidarity of the society is reaffirmed by everyone taking part in the preparations, and in Turkey the body is carried to the cemetery by all the men in the village. A wooden casket, which is usually not buried with the body, appears to float above the group as each man tries to carry part of the weight for at least a few minutes. The open house which follows the funeral ensures that the relatives will not be left alone. In Turkey this trauma can be so severe that a person may lose his mind. When someone has died, it is customary to say to close relatives a phrase which means generally, "let your head be healthy." These observances are intended to help the family reestablish itself and begin a new life.

The forms of distribution of property, obligations and prerogatives vary considerably from place to place, but generally a division is made among the sons. Women are said to inherit property, but they frequently relinquish these rights, for different reasons in different places. In Demirciler, Turkey, girls inherit equally with men, but they usually give up their shares, because "they would not want to take anything from their brothers," as one informant put it. Among Bedouin tribes in north Syria the women do not take their inheritance because it would "shame" a man if his wife came to him with money or property. These traditions, however, are not always followed. Schurman summarizes the Koranic provisions for inheritance: "The principal criterion of inheritance is consanguinity in the uninterrupted paternal line (*nasab*). . . . The male child always receives the double share. . . . The parents' share is an absolute sixth of the estate. . . ."[47] Schurman then lists a number of special situations such as for a man without any children. In Turkey men and women inherit equally in theory, but the males inherit all in practice. The same is true for Bedouin Arabs, according to one of my informants. Schurman says that "most informants agreed that women rarely inherit land, and receive shares largely in the form of movable property, like clothes and household goods . . . a woman usually turned her property over to her husband . . . and plays only a small role in the total inheritance structure."[48] Among the Basseri of Persia a male heir is given his share of the estate at the time of his marriage. If there are five sons he receives onefifth of his father's possesssions at the time; if there are three sons, one-third, and so on, and at death whatever remains is divided equally among the sons still living at home.[49] Thus it can be seen that property is divided more or less equally among the male heirs with provision made for the spouse or mother of the dead man. However, the practices differ from Koranic injunction because women almost universally "give up" their share of the property. The way these important events are observed or celebrated sets the Middle East off from other areas. Note, for example, the vast difference between American births in hospitals and those of the village or nomadic peoples in the Middle East, and the simplicity of a marriage by a justice of the peace, or even the elaborate wedding of a debutante, compared with the week- or two-week celebration in the Middle East.

The shift from rural to urban society is partly responsible for this difference. Urbanization has a tendency to rationalize institutions. Most of the ceremonies in traditional societies are non-rational, and urbanization seems to dehumanize the society. All non-urban peoples have ceremonies which fill a basic emotional need. An emotional deprivation may be the cause of many of the ills in modern society, such as juvenile delinquency.

Deep emotional satisfaction comes from the uncritical belonging to a group and the acceptance of standards set by that group whether they are rational or not. Najafi says, "It is no accident that family ties are so tight in my country. It is hours like these (during evening prayer, etc.) that the cords are wrought—sweet quiet hours. . . ."[50] In discussing her feelings one evening during Ramadan, when she listened to her brother sing a religious song in the village, she continued, "At that moment the deep meaning of the words [of the song] . . . the simplicity of the way of life that I had adopted . . . combined to produce in me the strangest emotion. The tears flooded my eyes, tears of happiness and sadness. All this . . . we must not lose for a sewerage system, for electric lights . . . not even for food for the always-hungry body of man."[51] This quote by a Middle Easterner eloquently expresses the importance that members of folk societies attach to the emotions wrought by their cultures. The intensity of these emotions accounts at least in part for the extreme conservatism of folk communities, because these people are loath to forego these emotional satisfactions.

CHAPTER SEVEN

Hospitality

One important ideal in the lives of Middle Easterners is hospitality. Gulick says, "Hospitality is a
virtue which the Arabs value very highly. . . .
At whatever time a guest may arrive . . . a cup of
coffee is made specially for him. . . ."[1] It is said of
a Basseri chief in Iran that, "his hospitality should
be boundless."[2] Barth says a strong Kurdish tradition
is "unending hospitality."[3] "May your table always
be spread" and "Arab hospitality is proverbial"[4]
introduce a chapter on this subject by Dorothy Van
Ess when writing of Iraq. In Algeria, "the hospitality offered to a stranger is considered inviolable."[5]
Such quotes are numerous, indicating that hospitality is extremely important. Western visitors are
constantly surprised when they stop to ask directions
from people and are asked into the homes of local
residents for tea and cookies. How many Westerners
would ask a stranger in off the streets, a foreigner
at that, to have tea? Hospitality such as this is
probably a result of centuries of isolation, an

151

important factor in fashioning the mode of human relationships in the area. Isolation is especially true for the villagers, and also for the nomads; though the latter travel extensively, fear of strangers keeps communication between groups to a minimum. The Middle Easterner does not fear four or five travellers, and welcomes these visitors. Tradition requires that they be protected, fed and sheltered for fairly extensive periods of time if they should choose to stay. The area under discussion is either desert or almost as arid, so that just staying alive is a major problem, especially when travelling. Small groups on the move need help and protection, and get it, unless they are enemies or mistaken for enemies.

Hospitality actually is the responsibility of the social group as a whole. Consequently, almost all villages have special accommodations for visitors. In Demirciler, Turkey, one large room of the home of the *muhtar* (local government head) was used for entertaining guests. Other villages have special guest houses, and among Bedouin tribes it is customary for the head of the local group to keep one room ready to accommodate visitors unless there is a special guest tent erected, including places for the guests to sleep, with the outside door always open. All who enter are served coffee, tea or whey made from milk, followed by a meal if the situation calls for it. The Kurds in southern Iraq "keep a guest house, in which the heads of families, all kinsmen, and any visitor have a right to sit."[6] In some areas this is "an institution of considerable economic importance, and a source of much prestige for the hospitable *Agha*."[7] Among the Marsh Dwellers of Iraq, "A village usually has one or more guest houses. . . ."[8] Each clan head, "should maintain a guest house . . . [and] is expected to be hospitable on all occasions."[9] In Egypt, "The hallmark of every clan is its guest house, where the adult members of the clan have their communal meals. . . . [and] receive a common guest. . . . "[10]

The extending of hospitality is tied up with the system of honor. It shows unselfishness, and sometimes wealth. It can be dangerous to refuse the hospitality of Middle Easterners because this offends their honor by indicating that you think they might not be good hosts or might harm you. Fulinain describes a meal served by a sheik of the Marsh Dwellers of Iraq.[11] A colored cloth was put on the floor and the meal begun by the sheik himself bringing the first dish. Behind him came a line of servants, each carrying two dishes. "Soon the cloth was covered with great mounds of rice, roast chickens, sweet pastries . . . and soon the whole floor was covered."[12] This is a display of great magnitude when one considers the critically short food situation almost everywhere in the Middle East.

Fulinain tells of three men who took a boatload of pomegranates across the marsh. On the second night they stopped and were given food by the sheik in whose area they were travelling, but when they had finished the meal, they were still hungry. One of them struck the empty platter with his hand.

This was an inoffensive gesture among the tribe to which they belonged, but in the tribe they were visiting it was regarded as a grave insult. The sheik asked them to come back the next evening and eat with him again. He had posted armed men around the camp so that the visitors had no choice but to comply with his request. When they "entered the guest-house" they saw "40 fishes" surrounded by baskets of bread. The sheik was there with his sword bared. If they failed to eat all the food they would be slain for having slighted the hospitality of the tribe. The storyteller said they ate all of the food and that more was brought. Knowing that their lives were in danger, they waited for the servants to leave the room, then they quickly ate the remainder of the food and threw the dishes into the river. They were saved because they ate all that was set before them, and apparently the host had no more dishes so that no more could be brought.[13] The fear of revenge undoubtedly would have a profound effect on the actions of people who believed that such things might happen, whether or not they actually happened.

Hospitality has a deeper meaning in the Middle East than in the West. Obviously the average Middle Easterner is not fully aware of what this pattern means to his society. One can get some idea of the difference between the Western and Middle Eastern customs by examining a few statements about hospitality. In Morocco, "only one person is supposed to portion out the bread at table. If anybody else were to cut the loaf again and to offer some more bread, it is thought to mean that a pretext for a quarrel is being sought for."[14] This is tied up with a widespread belief that bread is sacred. The custom of picking up a slice of bread (actually bread is broken rather than sliced by most villagers, as many feel that it would be a sin to cut bread) and kissing it is very widespread.[15] In Turkey bread receives the same kind of respect accorded old persons. "The laws of hospitality, particularly with respect to the sharing of food and water, [are] perhaps the most important obligation in the Islamic creed . . . stinginess, about sharing food . . . is damned by both men and God . . . a refusal to accept the offer of food is a grave insult."[16] With this fact so obvious to anyone who has visited the area, the number of books about the region which fail even to mention it is surprising.

This hospitality tradition can best be understood as an integral part of the intense struggle for prestige. Social interaction is frequently a set of stylized relationships, quite different from our American attitude, "Be yourself and if people don't approve, it is too bad." This pattern in the Middle East appears to be very rigid: ". . . Our civilization uses language excessively and even thoughtlessly . . . " but Middle Eastern society "makes a . . . controlled use of it, forbids people to talk indiscriminately on any subject . . . verbal manifestations of feeling are limited to certain occasions and then can be repeated only in the form prescribed by the social culture. Here, then, takes shape a way of life . . . based on a modesty

which hides . . . one's true nature and . . . prizes
the pleasures of the formal word and the measured
gesture above the search for novel expressions and
effective actions."[17] "Honor" is all important. If
a family has a stupid fellow in its midst, he can be
made to look reasonably normal as long as the
formal patterns are followed. This total restraint is
not placed on the head of the social group unless he
feels that he is at a disadvantage, in which case he
may protect himself by using only the standard
phrases and following the code of etiquette to its
extreme. On the other hand, if he can raise his
status in the eyes of others by breaking the formal
limitations, he is likely to do it, but only if he is a
leader such as the head of a family competing with
the head of another family. Thus deviations from
the formalities are almost universally interpreted as
a challenge to the other person, and as affecting the
other group involved. It is assumed that you know
how to act and are breaking the rules in an attempt
to show yourself (and your family, tribe, etc.) off to
the disadvantage of the other group.

For the Basseri, "contacts between chiefs . . .
are . . . of great importance. . . . Such state visits
are the occasion for much formality and conspicuous
consumption and considerable stereotyped rivalry. It
is regarded as important on such occasions to supply
lavish hospitality. Enormous traditional guest
tents . . . are erected. . . . Such feasts are regarded by the tribesmen as the high points in
nomadic life. Various opportunities are offered for
the expression of rivalry and claims of status by

guest and host."[18] Barth tells of reports by tribesmen
wherein the Basseri chief did things that no "really
hospitable" (in the Western sense of the word)
person would have done, such as keeping a guest
waiting for over two hours just to show that he was
not afraid to do it.[19] The chief challenged the other
chief; he knew the rules but was purposely breaking
them. This was in effect a restatement of the ranking
that existed between the two social groups. The
Basseri chief was goading the other chief to dare to
change his inferior status. Historically, these
rankings result from carefully balanced sources of
power. On many occasions the lower man has
accepted the challenge and inter-tribal war has
ensued, continuing until a new balance was es-
tablished or the old one upheld.

Turning to the hospitality of less important individuals as illustrated by my own experiences in
Turkey, I saw what Westerners would call "real
hospitality." Shortly after we moved into our first
apartment in Ankara, the mother and daughter in
the apartment next door came over with gifts of
food and offers to loan us anything in the nature of
household goods that we might need, since we were
foreigners and had just arrived with a small number
of possessions. This was a courtesy extended to us
with no thought of reciprocation. It involved only
the women, however. I never saw men extending
this sort of neighborliness except on one or two
occasions when the men were married to Western
wives. As an example of hospitality, my wife and I
were invited one evening to the home of a fellow

teacher at the college where we both worked. The
meal started with a bowl for each person almost
filled with a mixture of meat and vegetables, with
two lamb chops on top. Then came courses which
included a large plate of about 12 stuffed grape
leaves (each about the size of an American hot dog)
for each person, a serving bowl of pilaf (rice, pine-
nut mixture), about a dozen *börek* (meat wrapped
in bread and fried), two very sweet and filling
desserts and a large tray of fruit. The quantity of
food offered nearly everywhere in the Mideast is
almost unbelievable to Americans and Europeans.
I ate so much that I was ill the next day, from the
quantity—not from dirty food, as is often implied
in situations of this kind, and I was hardly able to
convince my host that I had had more than enough.
The members of the family of this young man ate
everything put before them. The significance of this
one meal can best be understood in terms of the
man's salary, combined with knowledge of his regular eating habits. His income was about $50.00 a
month, and he probably consumed more food that
one evening than he normally would have eaten in
several days. On an average day he would have had
tea, a small piece of white cheese and perhaps some
ripe olives for breakfast; for lunch some fruit or a
vegetable and half a loaf of bread. For dinner he
would have had mostly bread, but one main dish,
probably of rice. If he were lucky he would have
meat twice a week, but he served three dishes with
meat that one evening alone. Considering the man's
meager salary, this was an extremely expensive

evening. We would have been satisfied with much less, but from his point of view he was gaining prestige by feeding us so well.

Turning to a village where the people are extremely poor by Western standards, we visited this particular Turkish village on a weekend, arriving late one morning. The noon meal was ready for us, consisting of a whole roast lamb, pilaf, stuffed tomatoes and peppers, tea and dessert. This was served to us in the home of the village headman, the *muhtar*. The same evening we went to a home in a neighboring city where we had another enormous meal consisting of seven or eight courses. That night one of the old men from the village asked us to go to his home for lunch the next day. This had obviously been prearranged by the villagers, and again we were served a whole roast lamb, large bowls of pilaf, yoghurt, bread and stuffed vegetables. The cost of these meals must have been very high, the big spread designed to show the ability of the village to care for its guests. As a Westerner, this worried me because I knew they would go with very little food, perhaps for weeks, to compensate for the excessive celebration.

In Iran, Najafi writes that once she arrived in a village with a gift of mutton for the *kadkhoda* (headman, *muhtar* in Turkish and *mokhtar* in Arabic) to distribute to the villagers. The *kadkhoda* "protested, as he accepted the gift, that no one in the village was in need. . . . They served me [Najafi] a glass of tea and as I put my spoon into the sugar bowl I discovered that it was filled with paper with a thin layer of sugar on top. They were so proud they could not have me know that this was their whole supply; they could not let me scrape a spoonful from the bottom of the bowl."[20] This type of "trickery" is typical because of the relationship between honor, status, and the ability of the group to accumulate surpluses with which to be hospitable.

An Iraqi Arab, as recorded by Mrs. Van Ess, murmurs, "May your table always be spread," after a good meal.[21] "From the humblest tent on the desert to the sheik's lordly pavilion. . . you can be sure of a glass of tea or a cup of coffee . . . or a sumptuous meal. No visitor, even the most transient caller, is allowed to leave without partaking of hospitality."[22] Mrs. Van Ess later describes a meal in some detail. "I can still recall my amazement at the quantity and variety of the food. . . . Each whole roasted sheep was embedded in rice, some of it flavored and tinted with saffron. . . . Chickens, either roasted or in stews, were much in evidence, innumerable dishes of various kinds of stew flanked the large platters. . . . Croquettes . . . some of rice, others called Kubba burghil. . . . The great stand-by dolma was there in profusion—grape leaves wrapped around rice and mutton, delicately seasoned, and cooked by steaming. There was stuffed eggplant, stuffed cucumber, stuffed marrow and stuffed cabbage. Cauliflower appeared in stews, or fried crisply. Great bowls of Arab pickles . . . yoghurt with sliced cucumbers and garlic, and fresh salad of raw tomatoes, green onions, chopped mint and parsley. . . . Big pitchers of buttermilk . . .

and at every place was a great round of fresh, crisp Arab bread. For dessert there were oranges, bananas and dates, and a soup plate apiece . . . of milk pudding . . . made with rice flour and delicately flavored with cardamon and rose water. There were other sweets too, made with date syrup, and an assortment of tempting pastries."[23]

In illustrating the hospitality shown in Turkish villages and cities, Persian villages, and by marsh-dwelling Arab tribesmen, nomadic desert dwellers and Iraqi cities, it is seen that the variety and enormity are similar in each place. It is not uncommon to be served seven or eight courses, each about twice as large as an average American soup bowl, topped by dessert and fruit, even in extremely poor villages. The quantities and varieties of food served would be a strain on an American budget, but in the Middle East, where starvation is not uncommon even today, they are almost incredible. Hospitality in America is based on an independent family unit, but in the Middle East it is the responsibility of the entire village.

The explanation of the excessive Middle Eastern hospitality seems to be that by giving more generously a group can demonstrate its superiority, in terms of unselfishness, productivity, etc., over other groups. The fact that this competition is omnipresent on all levels should be kept in mind in attempting to understand the customs of Middle Eastern peoples.

CHAPTER EIGHT

Material Aspects of Culture

Thus far we have been concerned largely with what anthropologists call the non-material elements of Middle Eastern culture. These include what is learned and shared by the social group under discussion, existing as ideas or values rather than material objects. Some scholars have contended that only the abstract idea of the object is culture, that material objects are never a part of a culture. Others seem to treat cultures as if they were only a collection of artifacts. Non-material traits are transmitted only by intimate contact between cultures over a long period of time. A non-material trait is an abstraction and must be observed by another culture which will then decide whether it is worth imitating. This is an oversimplification, but it should serve to illustrate the difference in the ways material and non-material aspects of a culture diffuse. The evolution or growth of a particular trait is much more restricted if it is material rather than based upon an idea. And some description of the material artifacts found in the Middle East is necessary for anyone who desires even an elementary understanding of the area.

The principal concern of this book is the explanation of non-material culture traits which affect the behavior of the peoples in the Middle East. However, these non-material traits are a part of the whole culture complex. This includes a large number of material objects (if one prefers, the ideas which the objects represent). Thus a complete understanding of the culture must include at least a glimpse into its material aspects.

In describing material objects, we shall begin with houses (more accurately, residences, since many of these are tents). The typical Middle Eastern village is a cluster of mud-brick structures. From these the villagers go out each morning to their fields, returning in the evenings. This type of community has been referred to by some scholars as a nucleated settlement. The nucleated settlement traditionally has been a protection against raiding nomadic groups, though it may well be just a cultural convention that has roots so far back in antiquity that no one will ever know the origin. In any event, farmers in the Middle East do not live on plots of land as do American farmers, and in many cases fields are so far from the village that it takes two or three hours to get to them. This means from four to six working hours are lost each day in transportation. Despite this handicap, even today the typical farmer will rarely move out of his village to erect a house near his fields although in most places the area has been safe from raiding nomads for many years.

The mud-brick structures in which villagers live are predominantly of two basic types: rectangular with flat roofs or square with domed roofs. These houses are made by mixing soil, water, straw and sometimes a little manure or cement if available and keeping the mixture in a mold for 24 hours. The mixture is then dumped onto the ground and baked in the sun for two or three weeks. Then the square or rectangular structures are built by sticking these bricks together with more of the material from which they were made. The walls are usually over two feet thick; the rectangular buildings have roofs which are supported by poplar trunks, from trees especially grown for this purpose in a grove near the village. Poplars are especially good because they have straight trunks and grow very quickly—in Turkey about ten feet in a year. The grove is carefully tended by the villagers as wood for construction of any kind is scarce. Trees are planted a certain distance apart—different in different places because of the climate—which is designed to facilitate maximum growth and minimum waste of land. Each year an area of the grove is selected and trees are cut from that section. For home construction the bark is stripped from the trunks which are then laid out on top the two walls at the desired height. Mats are then placed over them and a layer of leaves covered with mud is packed on so that it will shed water. In heavy rains, however, these will melt.

Once our maid did not show up for work, and

when asked what had happened, she replied, "my house melted." We had had very heavy rains the day before, and not only had the roof dissolved in the downpour but most of one wall also. She and her two sons-in-law had spent the next day rebuilding. When a wall is completed the interior and exterior surfaces may be whitewashed if the owner can afford it, and when this is done the interiors are cheerful and attractive.

The square houses having dome-shaped roofs are made entirely of mud bricks, the roof being made of the same materials as the walls. The dome is formed by erecting a wooden frame, fitting the mud bricks on it and finally removing the scaffolding, leaving the bricks to hold themselves in place by their arch. This is very efficient construction in an area where wood is scarce, because the same scaffolding will build many houses.

Except for relatively modern construction, city houses are built in much the same way as village homes, but frequently have two floors. Some villagers also have two floors in their homes with the animals occupying the lower story in winter. Inside these houses, the floors are generally of packed mud covered with a thin, hand-woven carpet which is called *kilim* in Turkish and something which sounds like *gleem* in Persian. This ruglike material is not carpeting, but is more like a heavy cloth which has been woven on a narrow loom from woolen thread. The thread is spun with a spindle-whorl (a toplike device which makes yarn out of raw wool). This work is usually done by the old women in the villages. The

rugs made from this thread are colorful and attractive but rather coarse. The yarn produced in this
manner is about the quality of burlap but a little
softer. The walls are decorated with beautiful pieces
of needlework, with much gold and silver thread
worked into the designs.

The number, shape and organization of the rooms
in a village home vary considerably, but almost
everywhere there is at least one room where only the
members of the family go. Here the women do their
work. There is also one room for entertaining guests.
In addition, a variety of other rooms, depending on
the status of the occupant, may be added to this
basic structure. A poor man may have only a single
room in his house with space in the yard where the
women can work, shielded by reed mats from the
view of strange men. A rich man may have seven
or eight rooms including sleeping quarters for each
of his married sons, storage rooms and a large place
for his animals in bad weather. Here we see the
interrelationship between aspects of the culture as
the concept of virginity dictates a special place for
the women to work which is separate from the men
while that of hospitality demands special places for
entertaining visitors.

In addition to these general types of homes, there
are various styles in special areas to meet peculiar
environmental conditions. In the Turkish mountain
areas there are a large number of roughhewn plank
houses which are two stories high with the upper
floor extending out about a meter beyond the
ground floor. On the inside they are very much like

the mud-brick houses except that floor, walls, etc., are made of planks. Another specialized type is found in the marshes of Iraq, sometimes built on an island made of reed matting. In this region all buildings are made from bundles of reeds. These plants grow in abundance in the marshy land, and are formed into bundles which can be shaped into arches to form the framework of the structures. The walls are large mats woven from the same materials and laid over the frame. There are a number of other types in the Middle East, but the square and rectangular mud-brick houses are by far the most numerous and seem to be the principal types throughout most of the region from Morocco to central India.

The basic home of the nomad is, of course, a tent which is divisible into rooms by using reed mats or strips of cloth, when and if the occupants feel this is desirable. All the tents I have seen were black and irregular in shape, the size frequently reflecting the status of the owner. This type is very common throughout the area, and is probably best referred to as the yurt-type: the true yurt being built on a platform of latticed sticks whereas the yurt-type is built on the ground.[1]

There are several variations of the yurt-type tent in the Middle East. They consist basically of a forked center pole which supports a bent ridgepole. The ridgepole is driven into the ground, bent over the forked center pole and secured to a short stick at the opposite end of the tent. The short pole is driven into the ground at an obtuse angle to the center one and held firmly by a short rope of goat hair which is then tied to a peg in the ground. Around this, in an irregular pattern, poles are driven into the ground, slanting out from the center of the structure, each secured to a stake to keep it from pulling inward under the weight of the covering. The structure is then draped with a *palas*,[2] a black goat-hair cloth woven very loosely to allow the circulation of air. Since rain is not much of a problem in this area, the tents often are not waterproof. The back of the tent, where the ridgepole enters the ground, is covered, but the front is open as the *palas* comes only to the top of the wall poles. As a generalization we can say that the nomad makes a simple framework of poles, most of which are not connected with each other, and this is covered with cloth, loosely woven from black goat hair. Partitions within the tent are made from this same black material.

Furnishings consist mostly of rugs, pillows and a few pieces of collapsible furniture such as a small table made of a large brass or copper tray on folding legs. The more permanent house-types usually have only a few copper and earthenware pots and a small wooden trunk in which to place valuables. Mattresses are always available in both tent and house so that guests may make up beds on the floor. There are also containers for the storage of wheat, oils, dried grapes, etc. The nomad differs mainly in having fewer solid items, little or no pottery, and more articles made from skins, such as water containers.

Cooking is done on a fire in the open or in a

29. Centuries-old tree spouting water from a spring inside its trunk. Springs and rivers are nonexistent in much of the Middle East, and the lack of water remains a fundamental cause of the region's material poverty.

30. Mud bricks drying in the sun. Homes built of these mud bricks are constructed around a wooden frame which can then be removed and used again.

31. Twentieth-century cave-dwellers, Ürgüp, Turkey. (This is a common solution to the problems of a region chronically short of building materials.)

32. Bridge in Anatolia known as Gözlü Köprü ("the bridge with eyes"). This bridge, built in the 13th century, is still in use.

33–36. Turkish peasants harvesting wheat. After it has been crushed, the unthreshed wheat stalks are raked down from the ring around the edge; the threshed wheat is then left to dry in the sun.

37, 38. Turkish wagons used to transport wheat and hay. Because these wagons have no springs, some of the wheat will spill over and be lost.

39, 40. Primitive mills, typical for the area, used to process corn and wheat. The corn mill and the wooden hut shown here are on the Black Sea coast, the stone flour mill in Turkey.

41. Communal oven. Bread is an important item (estimated at 70 per cent of the total diet) for most Middle Easterners.

family than the villager. With the development of petroleum resources in the Middle East, one sees more small, single-burner portable kerosene stoves, which give a hot flame for cooking. But with kerosene suppliers widely scattered, these are not used often.

The village home, in addition to household utensils, has the implements necessary for planting and harvesting the crops. These vary from village to village or tribal group to tribal group, depending on the main sources of food. There are several varieties of wooden plows to turn the soil for planting wheat, rye or barley. These usually consist of a roughly shaped tree trunk for the tongue which is harnessed to the oxen by a yoke made of a heavy wooden beam with four wooden pegs driven through it. Two branches are used for handles and a fire-hardened part of the trunk sharpened to make the plowshare. The tips are sometimes reinforced with iron, making a much better plow. The ground is usually plowed in rows going one way, and the field then cross-plowed. Seeds are broadcast by hand, and a heavy log is dragged over the field to break up the clods and cover the seeds.

When wheat is grown and beginning to turn brown, it is cut with a hand sickle and piled up in mounds to dry. After drying, it is hauled to the threshing area on ox-carts made of wood or with a small amount of iron. These vehicles have no springs so that much grain is jarred from the husks and lost on the way to the village.

There are several primitive methods of threshing,

all of which involve crushing the grain from its husk by running something over it. The simplest method is by driving animals over the stalks of wheat, barley or rye so that the animals' hooves crush the ripened grain. A better method consists of pulling a threshing sled, which looks like a toboggan, but has tiny flakes of obsidian or flint imbedded in the bottom, over the wheat to cut up the husks and stalks. A somewhat more advanced machine is a vehicle with knives affixed to its wheels which serve the same purpose as the obsidian flakes. Associated tools include a number of wooden rakes and pitchforks, mostly carved by hand. Some of these implements are being mass-produced in the larger settlements now.

The age-old process of tossing the mixture into the air and letting the wind blow away the chaff is still used. In recent years small portable threshing machines have been used. These are extremely practical, as they can be carried by four men to the fields, and are powered by a man turning a crank. If the grain is threshed in or near the fields with this machine, the farmer realizes almost 100 per cent of the yield. This situation applies to most of central Anatolia, which raises the great bulk of Turkish wheat. Many large estates and government-owned farms have, of course, the latest in farm machinery. The portable thresher has the advantage of being cheap enough to be purchased by a villager, can be produced locally and is simple enough for an illiterate peasant to operate.

Time is not an important factor in the Middle

East. Most of the peasants work very hard for only a short season (except in Egypt) and are idle much of the remainder of the year. Once the crops are in, there is little for them to do.

The grain is stored in the houses in bags or pottery jars until it is ground. Grinding is sometimes done by the women of a family, but the grain may be taken to a mill. For the most part, these mills are very simple devices consisting of one stationary stone, shaped like a doughnut, with another one resting on top which is usually turned by water power transmitted to this movable circle of stone by a wooden shaft which comes up through the hole in the center of the stationary one. Some in Turkey were made with a wagon tongue affixed to the movable upper stone so that it could be harnessed to a team of oxen. One particular machine I saw was being turned by four women pushing at the point at which the oxen should have been harnessed. This type of mill is also used in Iran.

A mill in Cappadocia had been installed in the ruins of a Byzantine cathedral. It was powered by an old-fashioned internal combustion engine. Much grain is, of course, still ground by the women in their homes with mortar and pestle, and small, hand-operated replicas of the larger watermills.

There are at least four widespread and ancient ways of making bread. The first and simplest is to use a flat stone set into or at the edge of a small fire. The unleavened dough is shaped thick. It is then baked by the heat of the stone until brown on the side, then it is turned and browned on the other side. A related device is a dome-shaped circle of iron which can be placed on three or four stones with a fire beneath it, or installed over a small pit with a fire. For baking on the iron circles bread is rolled out with a thin wooden rolling pin about one inch in diameter, to a thickness of less than one-eighth of an inch, and dry-fried on the hot dome of metal.

In addition to these two frying techniques there are at least two methods of baking bread. The first and most common is in a circular pit oven about 18 inches across and 30 inches deep. It is lined with stones and is first heated by a large fire. When the fire has died down, the small pancake-like loaves are stuck to the sides of the pit and a heavy, flat rock is placed over the opening to hold in the heat. This is a very effective oven. A similar, but much larger device, found in many places, is an arched cavity on a flat stone base with a small chimney at one end and an opening about 10 to 15 inches high at the other. Charcoal, dung fuel, wood or almost anything that will burn is put in the oven and set afire. When the fuel has been burned, the ashes are removed, and bread, lambs, or anything else small enough to be placed inside can be baked by closing the opening with a large stone and covering the top of the chimney to hold in the heat.

Manure is an important fuel in the Middle East. It is almost never used as a fertilizer, as one might expect in this barren land, because of the extreme shortage of fuels. Any burnable materials are precious because of the scarcity and the scanty vegetation in a semi-arid region. People live for the most part in unheated houses, winter and summer. Despite the present abundance of oil in the area, comparatively little is consumed by the local population. One reason is the lack of a distribution system. Another is that most is exported. Homes are made with very thick walls which hold in what little heat there is. Fires are built only for cooking in most cases; if the temperature gets very low a small fire will keep the structure warm enough to prevent the occupants from freezing. Despite the common view of the Middle East as a place of hot, dry deserts, it gets very cold in many regions in the winter because of the high altitudes. The deserts are mostly mountain or rock, rather than the rolling sands of the Sahara which Westerners usually think of when they picture an Arab on camel-back wending his way across the vast desert wastes. In Demirciler, Turkey, at an altitude of well over 3,000 feet, the men used to gather in the house of the *muhtar* on cold winter evenings. His living room was heated by a small fireplace, an economical arrangement, as all of the men in the village could be warmed by a single fire. The only fuel generally available to villages is dung, usually gathered by pre-adolescent girls and shaped into small patties by them and placed in the sun to dry. Frequently these patties are stuck onto walls around the yard, with the imprint of five small fingers and a palm on each patty.

Other fuels available in smaller quantities are small sticks of wood, gathered by the old women foraging on the hillsides surrounding the villages, and charcoal, which is bought in the towns and is very expensive. To conserve these costly and scarce supplies, the people usually bake large quantities of bread at one time. The women in a village may hold periodic baking bees at which enough bread is made to supply the entire village for over a month.

Cereal foods must be supplemented by meats and vegetables. Villagers in the Middle East produce a wide variety of very high quality vegetables, but these must be irrigated to grow in the hot, dry climate. The average peasant eats a considerable quantity of peppers, squash, tomatoes, cucumbers, eggplant and cabbage in season. They have no way of preserving most of these foods, and as a result do without them when they are not in season. Other items important to the economy are grapes, olives, dates and a wide variety of melons. Some of these items can be preserved by drying, and keep fairly well for a reasonable length of time. In some extremely dry areas grapes are kept from July until November just by hanging them on a rack. They were slightly shrivelled by the loss of some moisture, but tasted very much like fresh grapes. Meat is always scarce among the settled populations because of the poor pastures resulting from the sparse rainfall. Thus the average person can maintain his life, but not at a high level of health. Middle Easterners are protein starved, usually eating meat only on ceremonial occasions, such as weddings and sacrifice holidays. Nomadic groups eat more meat per capita than do villagers because their possessions are largely in livestock. However, they do eat much the same foods and obtain grains, fruits and vegetables by trading their surplus animals, usually at a regional market, but occasionally directly with villagers.

These exchanges take place at a specified time for many of the nomadic groups which hold roundups at the end of the season when the grass has stopped growing and the animals would starve to death if the tribesmen tried to keep them. These surpluses are usually sold to animal buyers from the cities for cash. Most of the tribesmen use the proceeds to pay off their debts of the past year to the travelling merchants who roam the desert in safety because they are so important to the nomad. Without their products life would be very hard on the desert, so these traders are traditionally protected.

The nomad's purchases are all on credit and the charge for credit is often 100 per cent of the purchase price. This accumulated debt is usually more than the nomad gets for his animals, with interest included, so the nomad just hands his money over to the merchant and begins the next year already in debt. Nor is this interest rate computed on an annual basis; it is 100 per cent even if the purchase is made only a week or two before the payment. Since the merchant must turn over half of his profits to the local sheik, the transaction should be considered as a system of taxation rather than usury when evaluating the economy of the area. The sheik must have financial support, and this is not too different from an income or sales tax. All cultures have ways of keeping the trade and money channels flowing, and this method has worked well in the Middle East. If it is changed by the pressure of central governments, the heads of families, whether extended families, lineages or tribes, must in some way accumulate large quantities of goods and money to discharge their responsibilities to the social unit. The present system is not likely to change in the near future.

In the past many of the nomads' needs for non-meat products were provided by tribute from the villages under their "protection," an old and honored system of legalized blackmail. However, the central governments have stopped much of this, and in some areas the nomadic groups are disappearing because they must have this tribute to survive. The grain obtained from the villages, whether by tribute or purchase, is ground into flour by the women and baked, usually on hot stones or domed circles of iron. These iron devices are carried suspended from the saddle of a camel, and are utilized by placing them on stones above a small campfire. The nomad's breakfast is usually a hunk of bread left from the previous evening meal and a few dates. The midday meal is the same, except that an onion may replace the fruit. Lunch is eaten on the move. The major meal is prepared and served after the group is settled for the night, and often consists of a one-dish, meat and rice or bulgur (cracked wheat) casserole with bread and occasionally a dessert followed by thick coffee or hot tea.

Coffee in the Middle East is different from

American coffee, being made by pulverizing the beans and putting the resultant powder directly into the water. The coffee with the widest distribution is known as Greek, Turkish or Arabic. This is made in very small quantities, about two cups at a time. Boiling water is poured directly into the cups, and the coffee is drunk, grounds and all. A second type is found among some Bedouin groups and is brewed in a very large pot. The container is left at the edge of the fire, steaming but not boiling. When about half the liquid has evaporated, which in the dry desert air doesn't take as long as one might think, the remaining liquid is transferred to a smaller pot. This process is repeated four or five times until the coffee is thick and syrupy. It is then poured in small quantities into glasses. Since it is very viscous, it stays hot for a long time, and one rolls it up and down the sides of the glass to cool it, sipping it very slowly.

The need for irrigation was mentioned briefly, and authorities believe that the size of the settlement group in the past has been limited by the water supply. Water is not thought of in terms of cleanliness, but as a necessity for sustaining life. It is used chiefly to irrigate gardens, for drinking and for watering livestock which supply wool for rugs, tents and clothing as well as meat and dairy products. In the area surrounding a village, one sees the irrigation canals, the size and distribution of which depend on the source and size of water supplies. If the water is the property of the village, each farmer has the full flow of the canal which permits the water to run into his private water-distribution system for given periods of time.

Various types of machines are also used to lift water when the gravity system won't do the job. An example is a simple water skin on the end of a long pole with a counterbalance. These are large enough to lift several hundred pounds of water at one time by having a walkway on top where two or three men could shift the center of gravity by walking back and forth on top of the beam. Another ingenious device is the water screw, which is a tube with a screw inside it. When the screw is turned, water is forced upward. Dozens of similar lever machines have been developed through the centuries. Many of these are still in use.

If the water supply is privately owned, as are the Persian *qanat* systems, the owner sells full water flow by the day or week, using essentially the same system as that used for the communally owned supply. These *qanats* are large pipe-like tunnels which sometimes run for miles from a spring in the mountains to a village. They take years to build, must have constant care, because they continually silt up, and require a large amount of capital to construct. Hence the owner and builder sells the water to the users. The cost of water may be as much as one-fifth of the farmer's total earnings, but this is not unreasonable when one realizes that if the water were not provided the farmer would be unable to produce anything.

The five essentials for the production of food are: (1) land, (2) human labor, (3) animal power and plow, (4) seed and (5) water. It does not seem unreasonable to most Middle Easterners that the produce from the land be divided equally among those who supply these things. Thus it is not uncommon to find one-fifth of the crop going respectively to the landowner, the workman, the owner of the oxen and plow, the seed supplier and the water supplier. Since the large landowner often owns the oxen and plow and provides the seed and water, he logically takes up to 80 per cent of the produce. The actual returns from the landlord's investment, however, may not be large by Western standards.

From a purely objective view, the Middle Eastern system is not unreasonable when one considers that social security is provided by the landlord and nearly all taxes are taken care of through this plan. This is not to say that current land tenure practices cannot be improved. But they are a far cry from the grossly unjust system of exploitation they are often claimed to be. Furthermore, changing this system of crop distribution is not going to change the lot of the peasant in the Middle East because his products must be siphoned off to feed the masses in the cities, and this will be done, if not by absentee landlords, then by taxation. It seems to me that the present system is far more equitable than most of the "plans" proposed for changing it. The basic problem in the Middle East is the low yield per acre, not the distribution of the produce. It is true that the rich are very rich and the poor are very poor, but if the wealth were distributed, it would make very little difference in the standard of living for the poor. The per capita production must be increased before the standard of living can be improved, and most of the schemes for development in the Middle East do not adequately take this into account.

One interesting device for timing the all-important water-flow used in the area is a small copper pan with two or three holes punched in the bottom. As a man opens the canal or *qanat,* allowing the water to flow onto his fields, this pan is thrown into a small pool of still water. It fills slowly, and when it sinks, a stone is placed on the ground beside the men who are timing the operation. Each property owner is provided sufficient water for a specified number of fillings and sinkings of the timer. The old men of the village sit around the hole to chat and see that there is no cheating on the timing operation. Life or death often hinges on what each man produces, and being short-changed on water could result in starvation during the winter months. Westerners often think these old men are just wasting time around the waterhole, but this is a critical function in the Middle East and as a result is delegated to the oldest and wisest men in the village.

One of the major problems in the Middle East related to the shortage of water is the poor pasturage in most places. It is so poor in fact that nomadic existence is the only way a large herd of animals can be kept alive to produce even the minimum meat requirements. The nomadic tribes produce large quantities of this critically short food by grazing the desert as if it were a great pasture. These groups seem to pose the greatest threat to stable national governments because of their defiance of the laws. As a result the central authorities are continually under pressure to make farmers out of the nomads. If the nomads are restricted, who will produce the meat for the area? Farmers would only produce more small grain and perhaps enough vegetables to feed their own families. Being settled, the herds would dwindle rapidly, and the already critical shortage of protein would become even more acute, possibly to the point where the population would be decimated unless meat were imported or some vegetable protein produced as a substitute. This program has been tried a number of times in different places in the Middle East over the past 100 years with the result that a few years later the decimated social group again became nomadic in order to survive.

The fact that the nomad uses areas that would otherwise be useless desert regions to produce meats which could otherwise be produced only in irrigated pastures, in a region already critically short of water, does not seem to be understood by many nations and leaders. Too many politicians, born and reared in cities or in much richer cultural areas, have no feeling for the nomad except that he points to the backwardness of his country and modernization will mean his extinction. He is not an anachronism but an integral part of a functioning cultural whole, and settling him on farms is not only degrading to him but also harmful to the economy of the area. Many persons would make the Middle East a replica of Europe, but this region does not have the climatic resources of Europe, or most of the rest of the world for that matter. The interrelationship (Coon's mosaic, discussed in an earlier chapter) of village cereal producers, nomadic meat producers and cities of skilled artisans functioning as a whole suits the ecological conditions in the Middle East.

It is laudable to wish to help these people raise their standard of living, which admittedly is extremely low, but millions of dollars have been wasted in the area already by trying to bring "Western civilization" to places where the climate is not adapted to Western culture. The worst feature of tampering with the indigenous system is that if the nomads are settled and the protein supply reduced, even minimally, millions of people may die because of dietary deficiencies. Many changes that seem temporarily to improve the situation may only destroy something more important in the long run. The settling of nomadic groups or, in some cases, even excessive irrigation could after a few years actually lower the standard of living rather than raise it. In some cases improved medical facilities result in the saving of an infant's life, but the infant may starve to death later. Periodic famine has kept the population "stable" for centuries, and no improvements will raise living standards unless the population growth can be controlled. The number of people in Turkey increased by almost 50 per cent between the last two censuses. Despite all of the economic gains, the standard of living for the average Turk has changed very little.

Farming in most areas in the Middle East (excluding Egypt) requires that land be left fallow for from two to nine years, depending on local conditions. Hence good land is always at a premium. The clusters of mud-brick buildings which make up the villages are almost without exception built on barren ground, a fact which disturbs many Americans. Westerners who have not lived in the Middle East cannot understand why homes are built in such undesirable locations. But, with good farm land so scarce, no one would want to waste it by building houses on it.

Turning to the clothing styles in the Middle East, a wide variety of costumes is worn. The most generally used item, however, is large billowy trousers worn by both men and women. These have very low crotches and are loose enough to permit considerable freedom of movement. They are being replaced in many areas by European styles or local modifications. In respect to footware, the pointed-toe, Arabian-nights-style slipper is common. Above the waist is worn a very loose type of shirtlike blouse, tight around the neck and wrists and with no collar. A heavy woolen vest is usually worn over this, as are coats and cloaks, the style varying in different localities depending on climate, occupation and the social status of the individual. Headgear varies from skull caps to turbans to the folded, diaper-like pieces of cloth worn by the Bedouin

Arabs. European-type caps and hats are also found, especially where the governments have instituted clothing reforms as a part of the process of secularization as in Turkey. Traditionally, each ethnic group could be identified by some element of its clothing such as a skull cap with a special design on it indicating that the wearer was a Jew. However, this practice is disappearing under the pressures of urbanization.

One interesting aspect of dress is that of wearing the family exchequer in the form of gold coins or bracelets. Middle Easterners as a rule do not trust modern banks, so the safest place for the family cash is on the bodies of the women. Local currencies are highly unstable, and gold is thus a hedge against the almost constant inflation which has run as high as 15 per cent per month over long periods of time in some countries. When a farmer sells his crops in the town or city for paper money, he immediately converts most of it to gold in the form of coins, bracelets or other types of jewelry. If he is rich, he will buy precious stones.

The sultan's treasury in Istanbul is almost unbelievable to Westerners, composed of rubies and other precious stones. This form of saving, on a greatly reduced scale, is used today by peasants and businessmen because it gives them a feeling of security. The women wear these jewels until the family needs cash for something, then one or two pieces are sold. Thus the valuables decorate the women as well as show the possessions of the household. This practice and the deep convictions underlying it make the adoption of a capitalistic economy very difficult. If a man accumulates a considerable quantity of money, he will likely invest it in items such as jewelry, automobiles and refrigerators which, with continued inflation, could grow in value. But he is unlikely to invest it in an industry unless the venture promises a high return within a short period of time. Hence the growth of industry is almost forced upon governments, whether or not they wish to participate.

In an area which has in the past traditionally engaged in raiding activities, weapons should be mentioned. Even today a man will often want his photograph made with his weapon in hand. Most heads of families that I knew outside the cities had at least one rifle which they would show off and discuss with great pride. In Kaman, Turkey, one of the better weapons was an old double-barrelled shotgun, vintage about 1910. These guns are usually very old. In movies taken just inside the borders of Afghanistan near West Pakistan around 1960, a man was shown hunting with a matchlock rifle. For those unfamiliar with matchlocks, they have a fuze on them which is lighted and the game must be held in the sights of the weapon while the fuze burns down to the powder and ignites it. Besides these weapons, there is a large variety of knives and swords. It would be impossible to describe all of these; they are used today chiefly to settle quarrels, usually matters of honor.

In conclusion, there are a number of aspects of the material culture which distinguish the Middle

East from other areas: (1) the relative scarcity of goods even among the settled populations, (2) the style, material and construction of houses, (3) the loose billowing garments which have the effect of desexing the wearer, (4) the tools utilized in agriculture and irrigation devices, (5) the array of similar copper and brass utensils used in the homes and (6) a variety of weapons widely distributed throughout the area. While these six aspects of material culture do not constitute a complete description, they do illustrate striking differences between the culture areas of the Middle East and those of Europe and Africa.

Conclusion

For a better understanding of the evolution of the Middle Eastern culture through the centuries, picture an area which is very stony with numerous high mountain peaks. The land is covered with sparse grasslands and an occasional tree, gnarled and twisted by the harsh dry winds. Temperatures may range from well below freezing in the winter months to over 120 degrees in the summer. There are no streams, rivers or springs, and even stagnant water holes are often more than a day's journey apart. The sun can be devastating in mid-afternoon and one can almost freeze to death at night. Further, it may rain only once or twice a year, and in some regions not that often. Sometimes the rain comes in cloudbursts, with the water draining quickly, precious soil with it. Probably 70 per cent of the land conditions would come under this description.

If you were a nomad, your homogenous group would likely consist of from two to five yurt-type tents, several other persons and some animals, usually camels, donkeys, horses, sheep, goats and dogs. The number and variety of these animals would depend on how dry the area was. If water was very scarce, the herd would consist of only camels with a donkey or two.

After a few days camping in one place, the animals eat the grass down to the roots, even in the spring, which is the richest growing season. Since the animals must have food to provide the necessary milk, cheese, butter, meat, etc., the group must move to survive. Then the question is which way to go. Assuming that it is spring and getting warmer each day, it is only logical to move the camp toward the snow on the mountains. Snow is water and the grass is greener where it is cooler and damper. Conversely, in the fall, it is desirable to move the camp away from the snow and into the warmth of the valleys. Ecology, naturally, is the determining factor in this movement. Where there are oases, small numbers of people can settle and grow sufficient food. But the oases are few and the major pasturage problem remains.

While on the move, one would see an unchanging panorama of rocks, hills and barren land. And every day the hostility of the environment is brought home to the wanderers. If on occasion they were to pass near a village, the encounter would likely be hostile because villagers are jealous of their precious water supply, and the herds of the nomads trample and destroy, even when they are not eating the farmers' crops. Some mornings groups wake up to find that a number of their animals have been stolen in a raid, almost certainly by a rival nomadic tribe. Hence they cannot trust even their own kind. To add to their woes, the tax collector calls on them, with a bodyguard larger than the group of nomads. These levies could well decimate their herds, and in this situation there is one alternative to starvation: take from some group weaker than yours. In some cases the nomads could demand tribute from villages, but often the only alternative would be to raid another nomadic group.

Attacking another band of nomads risks the possibility of reprisal raids, to say nothing of the dangers inherent in the raiding. In determining which nomadic band to attack, the leaders would consider the possible consequences. Obviously they would raid the weaker groups. If they feared a group, they would respect that group and thus honor it.

All this emphasizes the importance of the male and the comparative unimportance of women in all matters bearing on survival except that of children. The direction the culture took was toward the glorification of such manly activities as fighting and bravado because they were assurance that other groups would not attack. With the men getting so much attention, it was only natural that the male children would regard themselves as the superior sex. With this sort of rearing the males cannot help being jealous and violently possessive toward their women. The women, of secondary importance, are isolated from other men to keep the jealous male nature from erupting into deadly rivalry within the group and disrupting the social order. The infusion of Western ideals in the last century has had the effect of easing the rigidity of this custom. The honor complex would seem to be a direct outgrowth of the system which treats males as more valuable than females. The separation of the sexes resulted from the jealousy of the overindulged males, and the emphasis on virginity is merely an offshoot of this.

The hospitality complex develops because of the need for small groups to be protected when travelling alone. It would be convenient to say that the earliest inhabitants of the Middle East were nomads and that villages developed when some of these people settled near permanent water supplies. But the earliest records refer to farmers in the area so that one cannot say with certainty that villagers are merely settled tribesmen. It is quite possible that primitive groups learned agriculture and formed villages, then when the populations became too dense, some of the peasants became nomads to relieve the food shortages.

In contrast with the nomad, the villager continually sees around him the same almost endless stretches of barren land. His village can maintain itself in this hostile region only because of a sufficient water supply. Since the peasant does not move around as the nomad does, his chances of seeing outsiders are remote. When outsiders do come to the village, they are likely to be nomads demanding tribute, raiding for booty or just damaging the crops with their herds. Non-nomadic visitors are likely to be the tax collectors from the strongest city-state in the region, an invading army or military leaders conscripting young men for the army. When outsiders come to harm the village it is the men who defend it. This has a tendency to over-emphasize, even exaggerate the masculine virtues. When a neighboring village needed more land, the men of that village would plant crops on adjacent fields if they were not defended. Nomads would steal produce and women if they were not defended. Thus, the ideal of the fierce, fighting male was furthered. The city dwellers too evolved a system of values centered around the fighting man or warrior, the subjugation of women and the enhancement of males, an unreasonable emphasis placed upon virginity, and a striving for status by excessive forms of hospitality. However, with the infusion of European and Western influences, many of the traditions which have served well in the past are now retarding the progress of the changes under way. I am not convinced, however, that many of the proposed changes are for the good.

One question has been asked me many times: Why are anthropologists interested in studying these primitive cultures which are so obviously inferior to ours? First, I would suggest that anthropologists rarely would say that these cultures are inferior in anything except technology. Different cultures result from adaptation to environmental conditions and to the history of the area in which they are found. One could legitimately ask, Why are we interested in these cultures now when they are

obviously doomed to change in the near future?
Actually little passes out of existence without leaving
its imprint on the next evolutionary stage. The
principal aim of anthropology, as I see it, is to understand the patterns of other cultures and culture
areas and compare them with our own so that we
can better understand why people do things the way
they do. It can be hoped that through an understanding of the Middle East, we can better understand ourselves.

If we look at the Middle East carefully, one of the
important things we learn is that nearly every
village and town has a different set of cultural rules
for maintaining order, and yet all are justified as a
part of Islam by the people who follow them. People
follow this course the world over, but this does not
make the social rules an important part of religion;
rather, the religion is important to the society because it gives a kind of rational base for irrational
behavor. That the present emphasis placed on
virginity has not always been a part of the European
tradition is clear from a statement by Havelock
Ellis that ancient Slavs would say to a bride found
to be virgin, "If you were worth anything, men
would have loved you, and . . . taken away your
virginity."[1] Then the husband would drive the
girl out as an unsatisfactory wife.

I would like to make it clear that the ecological
conditions in the Middle East did not predestine
the development of the cultural themes discussed
in this book. Rather, I wish to convey the point that
this was one of a number of natural ways the cultures

could have gone. They undoubtedly took this route because of certain cultural antecedents and continued along this way and elaborated on these themes because the cultures which did accept these values were more successful in coping with the environment.

In characterizing the area one is forced to note the harsh basic factor of poverty. This is related to the limited materials available for the people, not a judgment as to their economic standing. Poverty in the Middle East is hardly understood, even in the poorer sections of the West. In discussing the material culture, we noted the small amount of goods owned by the average family. Part of the reason is that nomadic peoples do not want to be encumbered with large amounts of goods unless they are things that the nomads really need. However, settled peoples also have few material possessions. This situation could be tolerated if the people were healthy, comfortable and well fed. Unfortunately that is not the case. As late as 1964 relatively few births were attended by physicians, and as a result the infant mortality rate is still many times that in the United States or Western Europe. Modern drugs are available only in limited quantities in some areas, so that the average life expectancy is still very short. Clothing, bricks and steel for construction are in very short supply, and the costs of such things are exorbitant in comparison with the annual per capita income. Fuels are scarce and in many places unavailable, with the exception of dung, so that it is impossible for the peasants to keep their houses at a healthful temperature during the long winter months, to say nothing of the retarding effect this has on industrial development. A few areas have vast reserves of oil, but relatively little is utilized in the homes because of the high prices Western nations are prepared to pay for it. Nearly all countries in the Middle East suffer from a shortage of foreign exchange; they need vast quantities of imports, but since they do not produce even enough for their own needs, they have little to export to other countries. Rising standards of living in the cities along with the growing expectations of the peasants make this problem more acute each year, and the population increase further complicates the situation. Food supplies are so scarce in rural areas as well as in the impoverished city areas that in bad years many persons starve. These countries have no social security, unemployment compensation, etc., because they do not have the economic resources to provide such necessities. Less than half the area's population has anything like a balanced diet, so that many fall prey to disease and many others suffer poor health. This may account for the lethargy of the average adult when he looks into the future and says "Insallah" rather than try to improve his way of life.

Under these conditions, is it any wonder that the peasant is pessimistic and suspicious, that he blames everything on fate (*kismet*), and lets events run their course?

Westerners generally have faith in the future,

believing that they will be able to leave a better world for their children. And experience has shown that for the average person hard work pays off in future security. Nearly all Middle Eastern youths who attend American colleges and universities catch this bouyant optimism, but when they return home they generally lose it and become embittered or revolutionary because they feel that things could be better if the rich would only invest their capital to build industries and create new jobs and services. This is in large part an illusion based on their experience in the Western world. Nothing the rich can do will change the harsh economic reality that in the Middle East there is always a shortage of almost everything. About all one can do in this situation is to redistribute the limited amount of material wealth so that different people become the wealthy or affluent, or that all people are poor. The wealthy, naturally, feel that the upper classes are more intelligent and thus more important than illiterate peasants, who understand little that goes on outside their valleys. They feel that helping these illiterates in a waste of time, believing that the rich are rich and the poor are poor because Allah so wills it. So the gap in ideology widens, and neither the young reformer nor the wealthy conservative fully understands the problem, and both become extremists in their own ways. The young turn to the power of the central governments in an attempt to uproot the cultural customs that are regarded as undesirable by the West. Unfortunately, Western leaders who seldom understand the ecological balance in the Middle East may inadvertently mislead these would-be progressives. For example, breaking up large estates may look good in theory, but large-scale operations are often necessary to increase production while small plots of land are not economical to work. Thus breaking up the large estates often reduces the standard of living of the peasant. In this respect, it is interesting to note that southern Italy has abandoned its 20-year-old land reform for precisely this reason, and this region is richer than most of the Middle Eastern areas. Fortunately, effecting land reforms in the Middle East has been difficult because the culture is geared to the ecology and reforms in many cases do not live up to the name.

The progressives rely on the authorities to enforce changes, but the power of the governments rests in the professional armies, for which most of the officers are recruited from the conservative classes. All this leads to the conclusion that true democracy in the Western sense of the word is almost impossible. The problem is centered in the conservative, inert masses of peasants, most of whom retain the picture of 7th century Mecca as an ideal way of life. Yet nearly all fervidly desire a higher standard of living. As an example of the thinking of many peasants, I recall riding in a taxi, and the driver pointing to a new building and saying to me. "See that? Next year we will all be rich." Not knowing what the structure was, I asked, "How?" "That is a new mint," he said. "Next year the government will print lots of money, and we'll all be rich." Incidentally, that is exactly what the government did, with the result that in less than a year the local currency dropped almost 100 per cent in value. This illustrates the level of economic sophistication that I encountered among illiterate people in the Middle East, and one cannot really expect more until the educational level is raised. Currencies are unstable and few will invest money in sound business ventures. This precludes industrialization at a rapid rate, where it might otherwise be possible. The peasants, while wishing to improve their lot, persistently resist attempts at modernization because it disrupts their traditional way of life. And the peasant usually votes conservatively on every issue except land reforms.

However, a trend toward a more liberal viewpoint can be detected, but this appears to be directly proportional to the amount of communication with the outside world (movies, radios, newspapers, etc., to which they have access; see Daniel Lerner, *The Passing of Traditional Society*, 1958).

The big drawback here is that progress is more likely to bring instability than stability to an already unsettled area, and no one really knows just what will happen when the centuries-old ecological ways are broken down. It is to be hoped that a better way of life will result, but there is no assurance of this, and it would be wise for Western countries to move slowly in pushing reforms.

One fundamental problem remains, and that is the lack of sufficient water resources. Unless the weather can be controlled and rain brought to the vast arid regions, the area will never be very productive. Irrigation projects can make limited improvements in some areas. The dispute over the waters of the Jordan points up the difficulties resulting from this acute problem. In ten years, if all of the proposed projects for diverting the waters of the Jordan are completed, there will be hardly any water left. These projects will increase production, at least temporarily, but serious questions have been raised about the wisdom of the projects in the long run. Large areas of the Lower Delta in Egypt have had to be taken out of production recently because of over-irrigation which salts the soil and leaves it unproductive.

Rising health standards have increased the population in some areas (Turkey in particular) by as much as 50 per cent in a decade. This increase was so great that many would have starved to death, even in the cities, in the winter of 1957–58, had it not been for large quantities of grain provided by the United States. Turkey traditionally has exported wheat surpluses to Europe. These exports enabled the relatively small number of city dwellers to maintain a near-European level of existence. This is still true because Turkey has in recent years exported its wheat for hard currencies and then received American wheat under foreign aid. This was paid for in local currency which could only be spent under provisions of Public Law 480 in Turkey for the improvement of the nation. This is in effect a kind of subsidy by the American taxpayer for the middle classes. But what will happen when the American surpluses are no longer available?

Population increase is an important world problem, but it is a critical one in the Middle East. When American aid is halted, as it inevitably will be, there will be critical food shortages throughout the urban Middle East unless the birth rate is drastically cut. For those who consider birth control a moral problem, I would have to agree that it is, probably the most serious problem facing the world today. However, I believe that those who are opposed to birth control are the immoral ones, not those who practice it. Many persons believe that birth or population control represents an interference by man in God's province. If one accepts this belief, he is committed to letting people die just as he lets them be born. The chief objection of some church groups to birth control is that it amounts to murder. I would ask, is it better to kill a sperm or egg or sit by and watch a fully developed child die of malnutrition? Even an elementary knowledge of biology tells us that every seminal emission results in death for two to three million sperms, and the continued life of only one when fertilization takes place. This is the work of God, not man. What difference could it make to God if one more sperm died in all that number? It is hard to see any sound moral ground for condemning birth control, and a great deal can be said for its morality. The preoccupation with the sin of sex has come into the Western world through Christianity from the Middle East along with the concept of virginity. The latter we have modified somewhat to fit our culture, and it seems that we must at some point stop being

hypocritical and alter the former by lessening our
preoccupation with the sinfulness of sex.

To recapitulate briefly, we have seen that a wide
strip of the earth, reaching from Morroco all the
way into the Punjab in India, in a great arc, including North Africa, Asia Minor and as far north
as Persia, constitutes a culture area. The cultures in
this region have a common quality, or flavor, which
contrasts sharply with Europe, Negro Africa and
other parts of Asia. One of the chief distinctions of
this part of the world is that it must be treated as
though it were three culture areas superimposed on
each other. The nomadic peoples constitute a sub-
area, the settled villages another and the cities could
be called the metropolitan sub-area. However, unlike
much of the world wherein sub-areas are separated
by different ecological conditions or geographic
boundaries, these sub-areas fit together in a great
"mosaic," to use Coon's term, and the societies of
each group are interspersed. To understand the
mosaic, we must also remember that there are a
number of different cultures, usually associated with
ethnic groupings, which are a functional part of a
whole in addition to the so-called sub-areas.

There are no absolute concepts of right and wrong
in the area, no crimes against humanity or the state,
but all crimes are regarded as offenses against the
honor of a particular group. Thus it becomes the
responsibility of every group member to punish the
offender if he can be found, but if he cannot be
found, then anyone in the offending group can
be punished. Much of the feuding in the Middle

East results from these long-standing disputes and punishments.

Group leadership revolves around the charismatic ability of a man to muster power in terms of fighting men. Decisions are usually unanimous and the status quo remains unless a leader is powerful enough to force his will on a group. The culture has a prescribed way of reacting to almost any situation, and the prescriptions are faithfully followed. Even a person of limited ability can pass himself off as a good strong member of his group by following the patterns.

Generally, man is a very social animal; much of his aberrant behavior results from not being accepted as a member of some group to which he would like to belong. He reacts as he does because a sub-culture to which he belongs, or wishes to belong, prescribes that if he does not act in a certain way, he will be excluded or at least criticized.

The Middle Easterner does not feel the sharp contrast between the natural and supernatural aspects of life that Westerners do. Much of what we regard as superstition is just as real to him as other aspects of life, perhaps even more real than germs, for example. It is important to realize this in dealing with the peasants.

Humans are the products of their culture, and every culture has a number of basic factors. To relate more effectively with people from another culture it is necessary to know as much as possible about their system of values. A further dividend from this is that we should learn a great deal about the disharmonies within our own culture which we can work to correct. To understand ourselves, or members of any culture, we must understand the motivations which drive races and individuals. When one understands the cultural milieu in which the Middle Easterner lives, he has gone a long way toward "understanding the Middle East."

Notes

CHAPTER ONE

1. A. L. Kroeber, "The Culture-Area and the Age-Area Concept of Clark Wissler," in *Methods in Social Science,* ed. by Stuart A. Rice (New York, 1931), pp. 248–65.

2. John J. Honigman, *Understanding Culture* (New York, 1963), chap. 1.

3. Joe E. Pierce, *Life in a Turkish Village* (New York, 1964), p. 29.

4. Najmeh Najafi with Helen Hinckley, *Reveille for a Persian Village* (New York, 1958), p. 97.

5. Carleton S. Coon, *Caravan: The Story of the Middle East* (New York, 1958), chap. 1.

CHAPTER TWO

1. Elman R. Service, *A Profile of Primitive Culture* (New York, 1958), p. 295.

2. Personal fieldwork.

3. Personal communications with Arab families.

4. H. F. Schurman, *The Mongols of Afghanistan,* Central Asiatic Studies, No. 4 (The Hague, 1962), p. 189.

5. Service, *op. cit.,* p. 396.

6. Najmeh Najafi with Helen Hinckley, *Reveille for a Persian Village* (New York, 1958), pp. 82–92.

7. Mahmut Makal, *A Village in Anatolia* (London 1954), p. 123.

8. John Gulick, *Social Structure and Culture Change in a Lebanese Village*, Viking Fund Publications in Anthropology, No. 21 (New York, 1955), pp. 81–89.

9. Najafi, *op. cit.*, pp. 82–92.

10. Service, *op. cit.*, p. 398.

11. Najafi, *op. cit.*, p. 83.

12. Fulinain (S. E. Hedgecock), *The Marsh Arab* (Philadelphia, 1928), pp. 59–61.

CHAPTER THREE

1. Fulinain (S. E. Hedgecock), *The Marsh Arab* (Philadelphia, 1928), p. 73.

2. Najmeh Najafi with Helen Hinckley, *Reveille for a Persian Village* (New York, 1958), pp. 89–92.

3. H. F. Schurman, *The Mongols of Afghanistan*, Central Asiatic Studies, No. 4 (The Hague, 1962), p. 214.

4. Dorothy Van Ess, *Fatima and Her Sisters* (New York, 1961), pp. 70–71.

5. *Ibid.*, p. 71.

6. *Ibid.*, p. 73.

7. *Ibid.*, pp. 71–72.

8. Fredrik Barth, *Principles of Social Organization in Southern Kurdistan* (Oslo, 1953), p. 72.

9. Fulinain, *op. cit.*, pp. 17–20.

10. Carleton S. Coon, *Caravan: The Story of the Middle East* (New York, 1958), p. 314.

11. *Ibid.*

12. Pierre Bourdieu, *The Algerians*, translated by Alan C. M. Ross (Boston, 1962), p. 21.

13. *Ibid.*

14. *Ibid.*, pp. 28–29.

15. Polygamy is now outlawed in Turkey, but some very old men had plural wives before the law was passed and hence some polygamous families are still to be found.

16. Barth, *op. cit.*, p. 38.

17. *Ibid.*, p. 69.

18. Bourdieu, *op. cit.*, p. 28.

19. *Ibid.*, p. 3.

20. Schurman, *op. cit.*, p. 188.

21. S. M. Salim, *The Marsh Dwellers of the Euphrates Delta* (London, 1962), p. 51.

22. *Ibid.*, p. 52.

23. Coon, *op. cit.*, p. 198.

CHAPTER FOUR

1. Carleton S. Coon, *Caravan: The Story of the Middle East* (New York, 1958), p. 193.

2. Pierre Bourdieu, *The Algerians*, translated by Alan C. M. Ross (Boston, 1962), pp. 97–102.

3. *Ibid.*, p. 97.

4. *Ibid.*, p. 98.

5. *Ibid.*, p. 99.

6. *Ibid.*

7. *Ibid.*, p. 100.

8. H. F. Schurman, *The Mongols of Afghanistan*, Central Asiatic Studies, No. 4 (The Hague, 1962), p. 169.

9. *Ibid.*, p. 170.

10. *Ibid.*, p. 193.

11. Fredrik Barth, *Nomads of South Persia* (Oslo, 1961).

12. *Ibid.*, p. 170.

13. *Ibid.*, pp. 11–13.

14. *Ibid.*, p. 25.

15. Schurman, *op, cit.*, pp. 52–56.

16. Barth, *op. cit.*, p. 44.

17. *Ibid.*, p. 52.

18. *Ibid.*, p. 56.

19. *Ibid.*, p. 2.

CHAPTER FIVE

1. Pierre Bourdieu, *The Algerians*, translated by Alan C. M. Ross (Boston, 1962), p. 3.

2. G. E. Von Grunebaum, "Islam," Supplement to the *American Anthropologist*, Vol. 57, No. 2, Pt. 2, Memoir 81 (Washington, D. C., 1955), pp. 111–26.

3. Bourdieu, *op. cit.*, p. 47.

4. For an example of what is meant by Folk or Tra-

ditional Societies, see Robert Redfield, *The Folk Culture of Yucatan* (Chicago, 1941).

5. For a discussion of urban culture, see Max Weber, "The Urban Community" in *Theories of Society*, ed. by Talcott Parsons, Edward Shils, Kaspar D. Naegele, Jesse R. Pitts, Vol. I (New York, 1961), pp. 380–85.

6. Carleton S. Coon, *Caravan: The Story of the Middle East* (New York, 1958), pp. 56–60.

7. S. M. Salim, *Marsh Dwellers of the Euphrates Delta* (London, 1962), p. 3.

8. Anne H. Fuller, *Buarij: Portrait of a Lebanese Muslim Village*, Harvard Middle Eastern Monograph Series, No. VI (Cambridge, Mass., 1961), pp. 5–6.

9. Daniel Lerner, *The Passing of Traditional Society* (New York, 1958).

10. Dorothy Van Ess, *Fatima and Her Sisters* (New York, 1961), p. 48.

11. Francoise Legey, *The Folklore of Morocco* (London, 1935), p. 121.

12. *Ibid.*, p. 126.

13. *Ibid.*, p. 153.

14. Najmeh Najafi with Helen Hinckley, *Reveille for a Persian Village* (New York, 1958), pp. 62–64.

15. Legey, *op. cit.*, p. 31.

16. *Ibid.*, p. 32.

17. Fuller, *op. cit.*, p. 85.

18. H. F. Schurman, *The Mongols of Afghanistan*, Central Asiatic Studies, No. 4 (The Hague, 1962), p. 253.

19. Legey, *op. cit.*, p. 33.

20. Van Ess, *op. cit.*, p. 149.

21. Legey, *op. cit.*, p. 35.

22. Fuller, *op. cit.*, p. 79.

23. Legey, *op. cit.*, p. 90.

24. Van Ess, *op. cit.*, p. 56.

25. Legey, *op. cit.*, pp. 109–10.

26. *Ibid.*, p. 200.

27. Van Ess, *op. cit.*, p. 153.

28. Robert Charles Albert, *Social Structure and Cultural*

Change in an Iranian Village, University Microfilms, Inc. (Ann Arbor, Michigan, 1964), pp. 926–29.

29. Mahmut Makal, *A Village in Anatolia* (London, 1954), pp. 86–87.

CHAPTER SIX

1. A village about 180 kilometers southeast of Ankara, at the south end of a large salt lake marked on the maps as Tüz Gölü.

2. Mahmut Makal, *A Village in Anatolia* (London, 1954), pp. 174–76.

3. *Ibid.*, p. 74.

4. Anne Sinclair Mehdevi, *Persian Adventure* (New York, 1953), p. 7.

5. Najmeh Najafi with Helen Hinckley, *Reveille for a Persian Village* (New York, 1958), p. 210.

6. Makal, *op. cit.*, p. 175.

7. Dorothy Van Ess, *Fatima and Her Sisters* (New York, 1961), p. 50.

8. Francoise Legey, *The Folklore of Morocco* (London, 1935), pp. 120–25.

9. *Ibid.*, p. 129.

10. *Ibid.*, p. 128.

11. *Ibid.*, p. 147.

12. Van Ess, *op. cit.*, p. 60.

13. Personal fieldwork.

14. Legey, *op. cit.*, pp. 147–155.

15. Anne H. Fuller, *Buarij: Portrait of a Lebanese Muslim Village*, Harvard Middle Eastern Monograph Series, No. VI (Cambridge, Mass., 1961), p. 35.

16. For a complete account, see Joe E. Pierce, *Life in a Turkish Village* (New York, 1964).

17. Legey, *op. cit.*, pp. 172–76.

18. Van Ess, *op. cit.*, pp. 60–61.

19. Fuller, *op. cit.*, p. 42.

20. *Ibid.*

21. *Ibid.*, p. 52.

22. Van Ess., *op. cit.*, p. 20.

23. Hamed Ammar, *Growing Up in an Egyptian Village* (London, 1954), p. 193.

24. Fredrik Barth, *Principles of Social Organization in Southern Kurdistan* (Oslo, 1953), p. 27.

25. Robert Charles Albert, *Social Structure and Cultural Change in an Iranian Village*, University Microfilms, Inc. (Ann Arbor, Michigan, 1964), p. 689.

26. *Ibid.*

27. *Ibid.*, pp. 691–92.

28. Fulinain (S. E. Hedgecock), *The Marsh Arab* (Philadelphia, 1928), pp. 197–202.

29. H. F. Schurman, *The Mongols of Afghanistan*, Central Asiatic Studies, No. 4 (The Hague, 1962), p. 205.

30. *Ibid.*, p. 198.

31. Albert, *op. cit.*, p. 696.

32. Schurman, *op. cit.*, p. 209.

33. Elman R. Service, *A Profile of Primitive Culture* (New York, 1958), p. 399.

34. Fuller, *op. cit.*, p. 193.

35. Ammar, *op. cit.*, p. 193.

36. Fuller, *op. cit.*, p. 54.

37. Albert, *op. cit.*, p. 696.

38. Service, *op. cit.*, p. 399.

39. Ammar, *op. cit.*, p. 200.

40. Van Ess, *op. cit.*, p. 41.

41. Fuller, *op. cit.*, p. 68.

42. *Ibid.*, p. 69.

43. Najafi, *op. cit.*, pp. 231–32.

44. *Ibid.*, pp. 215–16.

45. *Ibid.*

46. Service, *op. cit.*, p. 400.

47. Schurman, *op. cit.*, pp. 241–42.

48. *Ibid.*, p. 243.

49. Fredrik Barth, *Nomads of South Persia* (Oslo, 1961), pp. 19–20.

50. Najafi, *op. cit.*, p. 39.

51. *Ibid.*, p. 45.

CHAPTER SEVEN

1. John Gulick, *Social Structure and Culture Change in a Lebanese Village,* Viking Fund Publications in Anthropology, No. 21 (New York, 1955), p. 101.

2. Fredrik Barth, *Nomads of South Persia* (Oslo, 1961), p. 74.

3. Fredrik Barth, *Principles of Social Organization in Southern Kurdistan* (Oslo, 1953), p. 98.

4. Dorothy Van Ess, *Fatima and Her Sisters* (New York, 1961), p. 102.

5. Pierre Bourdieu, *The Algerians,* translated by Alan C. M. Ross (Boston, 1958), p. 28.

6. Barth, *op. cit.,* (1953), pp. 103–4.

7. *Ibid.,* p. 104.

8. S. M. Salim, *Marsh Dwellers of the Euphrates Delta* (London, 1962), p. 12.

9. *Ibid.,* p. 35.

10. Hamed Ammar, *Growing Up in an Egyptian Village* (London, 1954), p. 45.

11. Fulinain (S. E. Hedgecock), *The Marsh Arab* (Philadelphia, 1928), p. 127.

12. *Ibid.,* pp. 127–28.

13. *Ibid.,* pp. 247–50.

14. Francoise Legey, *The Folklore of Morocco* (London, 1935), p. 246.

15. *Ibid.,* p. 246, as well as personal fieldwork.

16. Elman R. Service, *A Profile of Primitive Culture* (New York, 1958), p. 396.

17. Bourdieu, *op. cit.,* p. 96.

18. Barth, *op. cit.,* (1961), p. 94.

19. *Ibid.,* p. 95.

20. Najmeh Najafi, *Reveille for a Persian Village* (New York, 1958), p. 5.

21. Van Ess, *op. cit.,* p. 102.

22. *Ibid.*

23. *Ibid.,* pp. 103–4.

CHAPTER EIGHT

1. H. F. Schurman, *The Mongols of Afghanistan*, Central Asiatic Studies, No. 4 (The Hague, 1962), p. 350.

2. *Ibid.*, p. 341.

CONCLUSION

1. Havelock Ellis, *Studies in the Psychology of Sex* (New York, 1935), quoted by René Guyon in *The Encyclopedia of Sexual Behavior* (New York, 1961), p. 254.

Glossary

Agha (Aga): title, roughly equivalent to English "Sir"

Allah: Moslem term for god, which, since Moslems believe there is only one God, is also His name

Anatolia: that part of Turkey lying on the continent of Asia, usually called Asia Minor by Westerners

blood feud: feud between two groups—families, clans or villages, for example—which erupts in response to a killing, and in which the offended group wish to sustain their honor by killing someone of equal status from the offending group

blue beads: small strands of spherical turquoise beads which appear over much of the Middle East as a charm to ward off evil

bride price: sum of money given to the parents of a bride and required by Moslem law for religious recognition of a marriage

camp groups: small herding groups, usually brothers and their families who live and herd their animals together

clan: group of people who, in theory, have a real or fictional common ancestor; actually, a basis for cultural regulation of the activities of group-members, such as marriage

endogamy: system of requiring marriage within the group

ethnic units: groups of people, such as Jews, Armenians or Turks, who consider themselves members of the same race

Evil Eye: a power, difficult to define, that causes sickness either through the eyes or by a compliment

Hac (Turkish spelling; Arabic spelling Haj): trip to Mecca to perform certain rituals; required by the Koran of all good Moslems at least once in their lifetimes

Hamito-Semitic: language family to which both Arabic and Hebrew belong

harem: women's quarters in a Middle Eastern home

henna: red dye used for beauty and in charms

Indo-European: language family to which Persian, Armenian, Greek, Russian, English and almost all European and some Indian (Indic) languages belong

Islam: name of the religion preached and created by Mohammed, preferred to the term *Mohammedan* by Middle Easterners, because it is free of the implication that they accept the prophet Mohammed as a god

jinn (often called genie in English): spirit living beneath our world, often in sewers, toilets and the like, which seems to have little magic power beyond the ability to cause illness and to change its form at will

kohl: black dye used in North Africa much as henna is in the rest of the Middle East

Koran: the Moslem Holy Book

life-cycle: anthropological term referring to the significant ceremonies of a society, required of virtually all its

members, such as birth ceremonies, marriages and
funerals

Mecca: Moslem holy place, Mohammed's birthplace and
still the center of the religion, located in Saudi Arabia

Punjab: large semi-arid plateau covering much of West
Pakistan and some of India and corresponding almost
exactly with the eastern boundaries of the Middle East
culture area

purdah: conservative Moslem practice by which women's
clothing covers them entirely, sometimes even to the
eyes

Ramazan (Turkish spelling; Arabic spelling Ramadan):
the most important period of the year, when all good
Moslems must fast during all daylight hours for a month

spindle-whorl: device, one of the oldest known to man, for
spinning fibers into thread

Turkic: pertaining to Turks, whether they are the tribal
groups far into Asia or those in Turkey

world-view: the way a particular culture sees the world;
a term based on the recognition that cultural systems
affect perceptions

Selected Readings

Barth, Fredrik, *Nomads of South Persia,* University of Oslo Press, 1961.

Coon, Carleton S., *Caravan: The Story of the Middle East,* Holt, 1958.

Fernea, Elizabeth Warnock, *Guests of the Sheik,* Doubleday Anchor Books, 1965.

Fulinain (S. E. Hedgecock), *The Marsh Arab,* J. P. Lippincott, 1928.

Fuller, Anne H., *Buarij: Portrait of a Lebanese Muslim Village,* Harvard University Press, 1961.

Legey, Francoise, *The Folklore of Morocco,* Allen and Unwin, 1935.

Lerner, Daniel, *The Passing of Traditional Society,* Glencoe Free Press, 1958.

Makal, Mahmut, *A Village in Anatolia,* Vallentine, Mitchell, 1954.

Najafi, Najmeh, with Helen Hinckley, *Reveille for a Persian Village,* Harper, 1958.

Peristiany, J. G. (ed.), *Honour and Shame,* University of Chicago Press, 1966.

Pierce, Joe E., *Life in a Turkish Village,* Holt, Rinehart and Winston, 1964.

Pitt-Rivers, Julian, *Mediterranean Countrymen,* Mouton, 1963.

Service, Elman R., *A Profile of Primitive Culture*, Harper, 1958.

Stirling, Paul, *Turkish Village*, John Wiley, 1965.

Van Ess, Dorothy, *Fatima and Her Sisters*, John Day, 1961.

Index

227

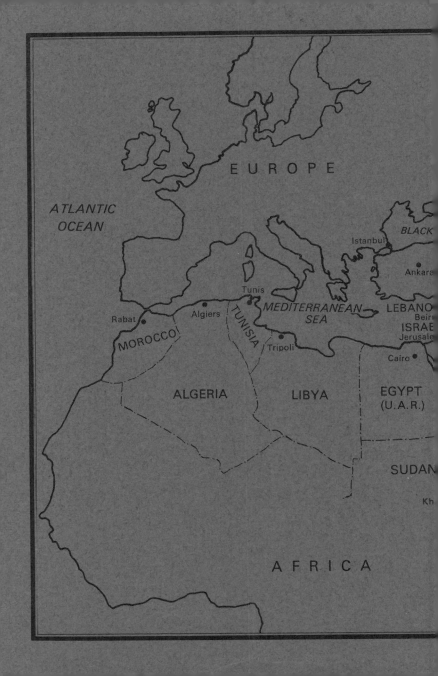